I0764242

J. G. Chapman, pinx^t — Copied from an Engraving Published in the New York Mirror. — A. L. Dick, sculp.

LANDING AT JAMESTOWN.

POCAHONTAS,

AND

OTHER POEMS.

BY

MRS L. H. SIGOURNEY.

NEW YORK.

HARPER & BROTHERS.

POCAHONTAS,

AND

OTHER POEMS.

BY

MRS. L. H. SIGOURNEY.

NEW-YORK:

HARPER & BROTHERS, CLIFF-STREET.

1841.

CONTENTS.

POCAHONTAS.

I.

Clime of the West! that, slumbering long and deep,
Beneath thy misty mountains' solemn shade,
And, lull'd by melancholy winds that sweep
The unshorn forest and untrodden glade,
Heard not the cry when mighty empires died,
Nor caught one echo from oblivion's tide,
While age on age its stormy voyage made:
See! Europe, watching from her sea-girt shore,
Extends the sceptred hand, and bids thee dream no more.

II.

Say, was it sweet, in cradled rest to lie,
And 'scape the ills that older regions know?
Prolong the vision'd trance of infancy,
And hide from manhood's toil, mischance and wo?
Sweet, by the margin of thy sounding streams
Freely to rove, and nurse illusive dreams,
Nor taste the fruits on thorny trees that grow?
The evil, and the sorrow, and the crime,
That make the harass'd earth grow old before her time?

III.

Clime of the West! that to the hunter's bow,
And roving hordes of savage men, wert sold,
Their cone-roof'd wigwams pierced the wintry snow,
Their tassel'd corn crept sparsely through the mould,

Their bark canoes thy glorious waters clave,
The chase their glory, and the wild their grave:
Look up! a loftier destiny behold,
For to thy coast the fair-hair'd Saxon steers,
Rich with the spoils of time, the lore of bards and seers.

IV.

Behold a sail! another, and another!
Like living things on the broad river's breast;
What were thy secret thoughts, oh red-brow'd brother,
As toward the shore those white-wing'd wanderers press'd?
But lo! emerging from her forest-zone,
The bow and quiver o'er her shoulder thrown,
With nodding plumes her raven tresses dress'd,
Of queenly step, and form erect and bold,
Yet mute with wondering awe, the New World meets the Old.

V.

Roll on, majestic flood, in power and pride,
Which like a sea doth swell old ocean's sway;
With hasting keel, thy pale-faced sponsors glide
To keep the pageant of thy christening day:
They bless thy wave, they bid thee leave unsung
The uncouth baptism of a barbarous tongue,
And take his name—the Stuart's—first to bind
The Scottish thistle in the lion's mane,
Of all old Albion's kings, most versatile and vain.

VI.

Spring robes the vales. With what a flood of light
She holds her revels in this sunny clime ;
The flower-sown turf, like bossy velvet bright,
The blossom'd trees exulting in their prime,
The leaping streamlets in their joyous play,
The birds that frolic mid the diamond spray,
Or heavenward soar, with melody sublime :
What wild enchantment spreads a fairy wing,
As from their prisoning ships the enfranchised strangers spring.

VII.

Their tents are pitch'd, their spades have broke the soil,
The strong oak thunders as it topples down,
Their lily-handed youths essay the toil,
That from the forest rends its ancient crown :
Where are your splendid halls, which ladies tread,
Your lordly boards, with every luxury spread,
Virginian sires—ye men of old renown ?
Though few and faint, your ever-living chain
Holds in its grasp two worlds, across the surging main.

VIII.

Yet who can tell what fearful pangs of wo
Those weary-hearted colonists await,
When to its home the parting ship must go,
And leave them in their exile, desolate ?
Ah, who can paint the peril and the pain,
The failing harvest, and the famish'd train,
The wily foe, with ill-dissembled hate,

The sickness of the heart, the wan despair,
Pining for one fresh draught of its dear native air?

IX.

Yet, mid their cares, one hallow'd dome they rear'd,
To nurse devotion's consecrated flame;
And there a wondering world of forests heard,
First borne in solemn chant, Jehovah's name;
First temple to his service, refuge dear
From strong affliction and the alien's tear,
How swell'd the sacred song, in glad acclaim:
England, sweet mother! many a fervent prayer
There pour'd its praise to Heaven for all thy love and care.

X.

And they who 'neath the vaulted roof had bow'd
Of some proud minster of the olden time,
Or where the vast cathedral towards the cloud
Rear'd its dark pile in symmetry sublime,
While through the storied pane the sunbeam play'd,
Tinting the pavement with a glorious shade,
Now breath'd from humblest fane their ancient chime:
And learn'd they not, His presence sure might dwell
With every seeking soul, though bow'd in lowliest cell?

XI.

Yet not quite unadorn'd their house of prayer:
The fragrant offspring of the genial morn
They duly brought; and fondly offer'd there
The bud that trembles ere the rose is born,
The blue clematis, and the jasmine pale,
The scarlet woodbine, waving in the gale,
The rhododendron, and the snowy thorn,

The rich magnolia, with its foliage fair,
High priestess of the flowers, whose censer fills the air.

XII.

Might not such incense please thee, Lord of love?
Thou, who with bounteous hand dost deign to show
Some foretaste of thy Paradise above,
To cheer the way-worn pilgrim here below?
Bidd'st thou mid parching sands the flow'ret meek
Strike its frail root and raise its tinted cheek,
And the slight pine defy the arctic snow,
That even the skeptic's frozen eye may see
On Nature's beauteous page what lines she writes of Thee?

XIII.

What groups, at Sabbath morn, were hither led!
Dejected men, with disappointed frown,
Spoil'd youths, the parents' darling and their dread,
From castles in the air hurl'd ruthless down,
The sea-bronzed mariner, the warrior brave,
The keen gold-gatherer, grasping as the grave;
Oft, mid these mouldering walls, which nettles crown,
Stern breasts have lock'd their purpose and been still,
And contrite spirits knelt, to learn their Maker's will.

XIV.

Here, in his surplice white, the pastor stood,
A holy man, of countenance serene,
Who, mid the quaking earth or fiery flood
Unmoved, in truth's own panoply, had been

A fair example of his own pure creed;
Patient of error, pitiful to need,
Persuasive wisdom in his thoughtful mien,
And in that Teacher's heavenly meekness bless'd,
Who laved his followers' feet with towel-girded vest.

XV.

Music upon the breeze! the savage stays
His flying arrow as the strain goes by;
He starts! he listens! lost in deep amaze,
Breath half-suppress'd, and lightning in his eye.
Have the clouds spoken? Do the spirits rise
From his dead fathers' graves, with wildering melodies?
Oft doth he muse, 'neath midnight's solemn sky,
On those deep tones, which, rising o'er the sod,
Bore forth, from hill to hill, the white man's hymn to God.

XVI.

News of the strangers stirr'd Powhatan's dreams,
The mighty monarch of the tribes that roam
A thousand forests, and on countless streams
Urge the swift bark and dare the cataract's foam;
The haughtiest chieftains in his presence stood
Tame as a child, and from the field of blood
His war-cry thrill'd with fear the foeman's home:
His nod was death, his frown was fix'd as fate,
Unchangeable his love, invincible his hate.

XVII.

A forest-child, amid the flowers at play!
Her raven locks in strange profusion flowing;
A sweet, wild girl, with eye of earnest ray,
And olive cheek, at each emotion glowing;
Yet, whether in her gladsome frolic leaping,
Or 'neath the greenwood shade unconscious sleeping,
Or with light oar her fairy pinnace rowing,
Still, like the eaglet on its new-fledged wing,
Her spirit-glance bespoke the daughter of a king.

XVIII.

But he, that wily monarch, stern and old,
Mid his grim chiefs, with barbarous trappings bright,
That morn a court of savage state did hold.
The sentenced captive see—his brow how white!
Stretch'd on the turf his manly form lies low,
The war-club poises for its fatal blow,
The death-mist swims before his darken'd sight:
Forth springs the child, in tearful pity bold,
Her head on his declines, her arms his neck enfold.

XIX.

"The child! what madness fires her? Hence! Depart!
Fly, daughter, fly! before the death-stroke rings;
Divide her, warriors, from that English heart."
In vain! for with convulsive grasp she clings:
She claims a pardon from her frowning sire;
Her pleading tones subdue his gather'd ire;
And so, uplifting high his feathery dart,
That doting father gave the child her will,
And bade the victim live, and be his servant still.

XX.

Know'st thou what thou hast done, thou dark-hair'd child?
  What great events on thy compassion hung?
What prowess lurks beneath yon aspect mild,
  And in the accents of that foreign tongue?
As little knew the princess who descried
A floating speck on Egypt's turbid tide,
  A bulrush-ark the matted reeds among,
And, yielding to an infant's tearful smile,
Drew forth Jehovah's seer, from the devouring Nile.

XXI.

In many a clime, in many a battle tried,
  By Turkish sabre and by Moorish spear;
Mid Afric's sands, or Russian forests wide,
  Romantic, bold, chivalrous, and sincere,
Keen-eyed, clear-minded, and of purpose pure,
Dauntless to rule, or patient to endure,
  Was he whom thou hast rescued with a tear:
Thou wert the saviour of the Saxon vine,
And for this deed alone our praise and love are thine.

XXII.

Nor yet for this alone shall history's scroll
  Embalm thine image with a grateful tear;
For when the grasp of famine tried the soul,
  When strength decay'd, and dark despair was near,
Who led her train of playmates, day by day,
O'er rock, and stream, and wild, a weary way,
  Their baskets teeming with the golden ear?
Whose generous hand vouchsafed its tireless aid
To guard a nation's germ? Thine, thine, heroic maid!

XXIII.

On sped the tardy seasons, and the hate
Of the pale strangers wrung the Indian breast.
Their hoary prophet breathed the ban of fate:
"Hence with the thunderers! Hide their race, unbless'd,
Deep 'neath the soil they falsely call their own;
For from our fathers' graves a hollow moan,
Like the lash'd surge, bereaves my soul of rest.
'They come! They come!' it cries. 'Ye once were brave:
Will ye resign the world that the Great Spirit gave?'"

XXIV.

Yet 'neath the settled countenance of guile
They veil'd their vengeful purpose, dark and dire,
And wore the semblance of a quiet smile,
To lull the victim of their deadly ire:
But ye, who hold of history's scroll the pen,
Blame not too much those erring, red-brow'd men,
Though nursed in wiles. Fear is the white-lipp'd sire
Of subterfuge and treachery. 'Twere in vain
To bid the soul be true, that writhes beneath his chain.

XXV.

Night, moonless night! The forest hath no sound
But the low shiver of its dripping leaves,
Save here and there, amid its depths profound,
The sullen sigh the prowling panther heaves,
Save the fierce growling of the cubless bear,
Or tramp of gaunt wolf rushing from his lair,
Where its slow coil the poisonous serpent weaves:

Who dares the dangerous path at hour so wild,
With fleet and fawnlike step? Powhatan's fearless child!

XXVI.

"Up, up—away! I heard the words of power,
Those secret vows that seal a nation's doom,
Bid the red flame burst forth at midnight hour,
And make th' unconscious slumberer's bed his tomb,
Spare not the babe—the rose-leaf of a day—
But shred the sapling, like the oak, away.
I heard the curse! My soul is sick with gloom:
Wake, chieftains, wake! avert the hour of dread!"
And with that warning voice the guardian-angel fled.

XXVII.

On sped the seasons, and the forest-child
Was rounded to the symmetry of youth;
While o'er her features stole, serenely mild,
The trembling sanctity of woman's truth,
Her modesty, and simpleness, and grace:
Yet those who deeper scan the human face,
Amid the trial-hour of fear or ruth,
Might clearly read, upon its heaven-writ scroll,
That high and firm resolve which nerved the Roman soul.

XXVIII.

The simple sports that charm'd her childhood's way,
Her greenwood gambols mid the matted vines,
The curious glance of wild and searching ray,
Where innocence with ignorance combines,
Were changed for deeper thought's persuasive air,
Or that high port a princess well might wear:
So fades the doubtful star when morning shines;

So melts the young dawn at the enkindling ray,
And on the crimson cloud casts off its mantle gray.

XXIX.

On sped the tardy seasons. Need I say
What still the indignant lyre declines to tell?
How, by rude hands, the maiden, borne away,
Was forced amid the invaders' homes to dwell?
Yet no harsh bonds the guiltless prisoner wore,
No sharp constraint her gentle spirit bore,
Held as a hostage in the stranger's cell;
So, to her wayward fate submissive still,
She meekly bow'd her heart to learn a Saviour's will.

XXX.

And holy was the voice that taught her ear
How for our sins the Lord of life was slain;
While o'er the listener's bosom flow'd the tear
Of wondering gratitude, like spring-tide rain.
New joys burst forth, and high resolves were born
To choose the narrow path that worldlings scorn,
And walk therein. Oh, happy who shall gain
From the brief cloud that in his path may lie
A heritage sublime, a mansion in the sky.

XXXI.

In graceful youth, within the house of prayer,
Who by the sacred font so humbly kneels,
And with a tremulous yet earnest air,
The deathless vow of Christian fealty seals?
The Triune Name is breathed with hallow'd power,
The dew baptismal bathes the forest-flower,
And, lo! her chasten'd smile that hope reveals

Which nerved the weary dove o'er floods unbless'd
The olive-leaf to pluck, and gain the ark of rest.

XXXII.

Pour forth your incense; fragrant shrubs and flowers,
  Wave your fresh leaflets, and with beauty glow;
And wake the anthem in your choral bowers,
  Birds, whose warm hearts with living praise o'erflow;
For she who loved your ever-varied dyes,
Mingling her sweet tones with your symphonies,
  Seeks higher bliss than charms like yours bestow—
A home unchangeable—an angel's wing—
Where is no fading flower, nor lute with jarring string.

XXXIII.

Another change. The captive's lot grew fair:
  A soft illusion with her reveries blent,
New charms dispell'd her solitary care,
  And hope's fresh dewdrops gleam'd where'er she went;
Earth seem'd to glow with Eden's purple light,
The fleeting days glanced by on pinions bright,
  And every hour a rainbow lustre lent;
While, with his tones of music in her ear,
Love's eloquence inspired the high-born cavalier.

XXXIV.

Yet love, to her pure breast was but a name
  For kindling knowledge, and for taste refined,
A guiding lamp, whose bright, mysterious flame
  Led on to loftier heights the aspiring mind.
Hence flow'd the idiom of a foreign tongue
All smoothly o'er her lip; old history flung
  Its annal wide, like banner on the wind,

And o'er the storied page, with rapture wild,
A new existence dawn'd on nature's fervent child.

XXXV.

A throng is gathering; for the hallow'd dome
At evening tide is rich with sparkling light,
And from its verdant bound each rural home
Sends forth its blossom'd gifts, profusely bright;
While here and there, amid the clustering flowers,
Some stately chief or painted warrior towers,
Hail'd as a brother mid the festal rite:
Peace waves her garland o'er the favour'd place
Where weds the new-born West, with Europe's lordly race.

XXXVI.

A group before the altar. Breathe thy vow,
Loving and stainless one, without a fear;
For he who wins thee to his bosom now,
Gem of the wild, unparalleled and dear,
Will guard thee ever, as his treasure rare,
With changeless tenderness and constant care;
How speaks his noble brow a soul sincere,
While the old white-hair'd king, with eye of pride,
Gives to his ardent hand the timid, trusting bride.

XXXVII.

Not with more heartfelt joy the warlike bands
Of Albion, spent with long, disastrous fray,
Beheld young Tudor cleanse his blood-stain'd hands,
And lead the blooming heir of York away,

'Neath the sweet music of the marriage bells;
Then on those tented hills and ravaged dells
The War of Roses died: no more the ray
Of white or red, the fires of hate illumed,
But from their blended roots the rose of Sharon bloom'd.

XXXVIII.

Young wife, how beautiful the months swept by.
Within thy bower methinks I view thee still:
The meek observance of thy lifted eye
Bent on thy lord, and prompt to do his will,
The care for him, the happiness to see
His soul's full confidence repose in thee,
The sacrifice of self, the ready skill
In duty's path, the love without alloy,
These gave each circling year a brighter crown of joy.

XXXIX.

Out on the waters! On the deep, deep sea!
Out, out upon the waters! Surging foam,
Swell'd by the winds, rolls round her wild and free,
And memory wandereth to her distant home,
To fragrant gales, the blossom'd boughs that stir,
To the sad sire who fondly dreams of her;
But kindling smiles recall the thoughts that roam,
For at her side a bright-hair'd nursling plays,
While bends her bosom's lord with fond, delighted gaze.

XL.

And this is woman's world. It matters not
Though in the trackless wilderness she dwell,
Or on the cliff where hangs the Switzer's cot,
Or in the subterranean Greenland cell:

Her world is in the heart. Rude storms may rise,
And dark eclipse involve ambition's skies,
But dear affection's flame burns pure and well,
And therefore 'tis, with such a placid eye,
She sooths her loved ones' pangs, or lays her down to die.

XLI.

Lo ! Albion's cliffs, in glorious light that shine,
Welcome the princess of the infant West.
'Twas nobly done, thou queen of Stuart's line,
To sooth the tremours of that stranger's breast ;
And when, upon thy ladies richly dight,
She, through a flood of ebon tresses bright,
Uplifts the glances of a timid guest,
What saw she there ? The greeting smiles that brought
O'er her own lofty brow its native hues of thought.

XLII.

But what delighted awe her accents breathed,
The gorgeous domes of ancient days to trace,
The castellated towers, with ivy wreathed,
The proud mementoes of a buried race ;
Or 'neath some mighty minster's solemn pile,
Dim arch, and fretted roof, and long-drawn aisle,
How rush'd the heart's blood wildly to her face,
When, from the living organ's thunder-chime,
The full Te Deum burst in melody sublime.

XLIII.

Yet, mid the magic of those regal walls,
The glittering train, the courtier's flattering tone,
Or by her lord, through fair ancestral halls,
Led on, to claim their treasures as her own,

Stole back the scenery of her solitude:
An aged father, in his cabin rude,
Mix'd with her dreams a melancholy moan,
Notching his simple calendar with pain,
And straining his red eye to watch the misty main.

XLIV.

Prayer, prayer for him! when the young dawn arose
With its gray banner, or red day declined,
Up went his name, forever blent with those
Most close and strong around her soul entwined,
Husband and child; and, as the time drew near
To fold him to her heart with filial tear,
For her first home her warm affections pined.
That time—it came not! for a viewless hand
Was stretch'd to bar her foot from her green childhood's land.

XLV.

Sweet sounds of falling waters, cool and clear,
The crystal streams, her playmates, far away,
Oft, oft their dulcet music mock'd her ear,
As, restless, on her fever'd couch she lay;
Strange visions hover'd round, and harpings high,
From spirit-bands, and then her lustrous eye
Welcomed the call; but earth resumed its sway,
And all its sacred ties convulsive twined.
How hard to spread the wing, and leave the loved behind.

XLVI.

Sunset in England at the autumn prime!
Through foliage rare, what floods of light were sent!
The full and whitening harvest knew its time,
And to the sickle of the reaper bent;
Forth rode the winged seeds upon the gale,
New homes to find; but she, with lip so pale,
Who on the arm of her beloved leant,
Breathed words of tenderness, with smile serene,
Though faint and full of toil, the gasp and groan between.

XLVII.

"Oh, dearest friend, Death, cometh! He is here,
Here at my heart! Air! air! that I may speak
My hoarded love, my gratitude sincere,
To thee and to thy people. But I seek
In vain. Though most unworthy, yet I hear
A call, a voice too bless'd for mortal ear;"
And with a marble coldness on her cheek,
And one long moan, like breaking harp-string sweet,
She bare the unspoken lore to her Redeemer's feet.

XLVIII.

Gone? *Gone?* Alas! the burst of wild despair
That rent his bosom who had loved so well;
He had not yet put forth his strength to bear,
So suddenly and sore the death-shaft fell:
Man hath a godlike might in danger's hour,
In the red battle, or the tempest's power;
Yet is he weak when tides of anguish swell;

Ah, who can mark with cold and tearless eyes
The grief of stricken man when his sole idol dies!

XLIX.

And she had fled, in whom his heart's deep joy
Was garner'd up ; fled, like the rushing flame,
And left no farewell for her fair young boy.
Lo! in his nurse's arms he careless came,
A noble creature, with his full dark eye
And clustering curls, in nature's majesty;
But, with a sudden shriek, his mother's name
Burst from his lips, and, gazing on the clay,
He stretch'd his eager arms where the cold sleeper lay.

L.

"Oh mother! mother!" Did that bitter cry
Send a shrill echo through the realm of death?
Look, to the trembling fringes of the eye.
List, the sharp shudder of returning breath,
The spirit's sob! They lay him on her breast;
One long, long kiss on his bright brow she press'd;
Even from heaven's gate of bliss she lingereth,
To breathe one blessing o'er his precious head,
And then her arm unclasps, and she is of the dead.

LI.

The dead! the sainted dead! why should we weep
At the last change their settled features take?
At the calm impress of that holy sleep
Which care and sorrow never more shall break?
Believe we not His word who rends the tomb,
And bids the slumberers from that transient gloom
In their Redeemer's glorious image wake?

Approach we not the same sepulchral bourne
Swift as the shadow fleets ? What time have we to mourn ?

LII.

A little time thou found'st, O pagan king,
A little space, to murmur and repine :
Oh, bear a few brief months affliction's sting,
And gaze despondent o'er the billowy brine,
And then to the Great Spirit, dimly traced
Through cloud and tempest, and with fear embraced,
In doubt and mystery, thy breath resign ;
And to thy scorn'd and perish'd people go,
From whose long-trampled dust our flowers and herbage grow.

LIII.

Like the fallen leaves those forest-tribes have fled :
Deep 'neath the turf their rusted weapon lies ;
No more their harvest lifts its golden head,
Nor from their shaft the stricken red-deer flies :
But from the far, far west, where holds, so hoarse,
The lonely Oregon, its rock-strewn course,
While old Pacific's sullen surge replies,
Are heard their exiled murmurings deep and low,
Like one whose smitten soul departeth full of wo.

LIV.

I would ye were not, from your fathers' soil,
Track'd like the dun wolf, ever in your breast
The coal of vengeance and the curse of toil ;
I would we had not to your mad lip prest

The fiery poison-cup, nor on ye turn'd
The blood-tooth'd ban-dog, foaming, as he burn'd
  To tear your flesh; but thrown in kindness bless'd
The brother's arm around ye, as ye trod,
And led ye, sad of heart, to the bless'd Lamb of God.

LV.

Forgotten race, farewell! Your haunts we tread,
  Our mighty rivers speak your words of yore,
Our mountains wear them on their misty head,
  Our sounding cataracts hurl them to the shore;
But on the lake your flashing oar is still,
Hush'd is your hunter's cry on dale and hill,
  Your arrow stays the eagle's flight no more;
And ye, like troubled shadows, sink to rest
In unremember'd tombs, unpitied and unbless'd.

LVI.

The council-fires are quench'd, that erst so red
  Their midnight volume mid the groves entwined;
King, stately chief, and warrior-host are dead,
  Nor remnant nor memorial left behind:
But thou, O forest-princess, true of heart,
When o'er our fathers waved destruction's dart,
  Shalt in their children's loving hearts be shrined;
Pure, lonely star, o'er dark oblivion's wave,
It is not meet thy name should moulder in the grave.

NOTES.

Stanza iii., line 4.

Their tassel'd corn.

To those not familiar with the appearance of the Indian corn, on whose cultivation the aborigines of America relied as a principal article of subsistence, it may be well to say that a silky fibre, sometimes compared to a tassel, is protruded from the extremity of the sheath which envelops the golden ear, or sheaf of that stately and beautiful vegetable.

Stanza vi., line 1.

Spring robes the vales.

The ships which bore the Virginian colonists—the founders of our nation—entered the Chesapeake April 26, 1607; and on the 13th of May, five months from the time of setting sail from England, which was December 19th, 1606, a permanent embarkation was effected at Jamestown, fifty miles up that noble river, to which the name of James was given, in honour of the reigning monarch.

Stanza vii., line 3.

Their lily-handed youths essay the toil.

"The axe frequently blistered their tender fingers, so that many times every third blow had a loud oath to drown its echo."—*Hillard's Life of Captain Smith.*

Stanza ix., line 8.

England, sweet mother.

"Lord, bless England, our sweet native country," was the morning and evening prayer in the church at Jamestown, the first church erected in our Western world.

Stanza xi., line 2.

The fragrant offspring of the genial morn
They duly brought.

" At the beginning of each day they assembled in the little church, which was kept neatly trimmed with the wild flowers of the country."—*Bancroft*, vol. i., p. 141.

Stanza xiii., line 3.

Spoil'd youths.

" A great part of the new company who came out in 1609," says the historian Stith, " consisted of unruly sparks, packed off by their friends to escape worse destinies at home. The rest were chiefly made up of poor gentlemen, broken tradesmen, footmen, and such others as were fitter to spoil and ruin a commonwealth than to help to raise and maintain one. 'When you send again,' Captain Smith was constrained to write to the Corporation in London, 'I entreat you, rather send but thirty carpenters, husbandmen, gardeners, fishermen, blacksmiths, masons, and diggers-up of trees' roots, than a thousand of such as we have.' "

Stanza xiv., line 1.

Here, in his surplice white, the pastor stood.

"The morning-star of the church was the Rev. Mr. Hunt, sent out by the London company in 1606, among the leaders of the infant colony. It was he who administered the sacrament of the Lord's Supper for the first time in Virginia at Jamestown, the first permanent habitation of the English in America, and the site of the first Christian temple. He was a man of a truly humble, meek, and peaceful spirit, and it is impossible now to estimate the value of the beneficial influence he exercised upon the fortunes of the colony. His kind offices as peacemaker were frequently interposed to harmonize differences which would have been fatal to the enterprise; and his example of suffering affliction, and of patience in sickness, in poverty, in peril, cheered his drooping companions, inspiring them with such fortitude, and stimulating them to such efforts, as, with the blessing of Providence, enabled them to maintain their difficult positions."—*Rev. Philip Slaughter.*

Stanza xvi., line 2.

The mighty monarch of the tribes that roam
A thousand forests.

Powhatan, the king of the country where the founders of Virginia first chose their residence, was said to hold dominion over thirty nations or tribes who inhabited that region; and being possessed both of arbitrary power and much native talent, his enmity was dreaded, and pains taken by the colonists to conciliate his friendship.

Stanza xvii., line 1.

A forest-child, amid the flowers at play.

"Pocahontas, the daughter of Powhatan, a girl of ten or twelve years of age, who, not only for feature, countenance, and expression, much exceeded any of the rest of her people, but for wit and spirit was the only nonpareil of the country."—*Captain John Smith.*

Stanza xix., line 9.

And bade the victim live, and be his servant still.

"Live! live!" said the softened monarch, "and make hatchets for me and necklaces for Pocahontas."

Stanza xxi., line 6.

Dauntless to rule, or patient to endure.

The extraordinary features in the character of Captain John Smith, and the strange incidents which made almost the whole of his life a romance, are exhibited by many historians. Hillard, in his biography of him, says, "We see him performing at the same time the offices of a provident governor, a valiant soldier, an industrious labourer, capable alike of commanding and of executing. He seemed to court the dangers from which other men shrank, or which they encountered only from a sense of duty. As the storm darkens around him, his spirit grows more bright and serene. That which appals and disheartens others only animates him. He had a soul of fire, encased in a frame of adamant. Thus was he enabled to endure and accomplish all the promptings of his adventurous spirit." "He was the father of Virginia," says Bancroft in his history, "the true leader who first planted the Saxon vine in the United States."

Stanza xxii., line 7.

Their baskets teeming with the golden ear.

When the colony was in danger of utter extinction from the want of food, her zeal and benevolence never slumbered. Accompanied by her companions, the child Pocahontas came every few days to the fort with baskets of corn for the starving garrison. Smith, in his letter to Queen Anne, writes, "She, next under God, was the instrument to preserve this colony from death, famine, and utter confusion, which, if in those times had once been dissolved, Virginia might have lain as it was at our first arrival unto this day."

Stanza xxvi., line 9.

And, with that warning voice, the guardian angel fled.

"Notwithstanding, the eternal, all-seeing God did prevent the plot of Powhatan, and by a strange means. For Pocahontas, his dearest jewel and daughter, came through the irksome woods in that dark night, and told us that great cheer might be sent us by-and-by, but that the king, and all the power he could make, would afterward come and kill us all. Therefore, if we would live, she wished us presently to be gone. Such things as she delighted in we would have given her; but, with tears running down her cheeks, she said she durst not be seen to have them; for, if Powhatan should know it, she were but dead. And so she ran away by herself, as she came."—*Captain Smith.*

Stanza xxix., line 7.

Held as a hostage.

The object of the capture and detention of the princess seems to have been to bring her father to such terms as the colonists desired, or to extort from him a large ransom; both of which designs were frustrated.

Stanza xxxv., line 9.

Where weds the new-born West with Europe's lordly race.

The marriage of Mr. Rolfe with Pocahontas took place in the church at Jamestown in the month of April, 1613, and gave great delight to Powhatan and his chieftains, who were present at the ceremony, and also to the English, and proved a bond of peace and amity between them as lasting as the life of the Indian king.

Stanza xxxvii., line 9.

But from their blended roots the rose of Sharon bloom'd.

The rose striped with white and red, sometimes called the rose of Sharon, has been said, in some ancient legend, to have been first seen in England after the marriage of Henry VII. to Elizabeth, daughter of Edward IV., when the civil war which had so long raged with bitterness was terminated, and the Red Rose of Lancaster and the White Rose of York ceased to be the unnatural symbols of bloodshed.

Stanza xli., line 3.

'Twas nobly done, thou queen of Stuart's line.

On the 12th of June, 1616, Mr. Rolfe, with his Indian wife, who, after her baptism, was known by the name of the Lady Rebecca, arrived in England. Her merits had preceded her, and secured for her the attentions and hospitality of persons of rank and influence. The queen of James I., the reigning monarch, treated her with affability and respect. "It pleased both the king's and queen's majesties," writes Captain Smith, "honourably to esteem her, accompanied with that honourable lady, the Lady Delaware, and that honourable lord her husband, and divers other persons of good quality, both publicly and at the masks and concerts, to her great satisfaction and content."

Stanza xliii., line 8.

Notching his simple calendar.

The mode of computation by cutting notches upon a stick prevailed among many of our aboriginal tribes. One of the council of Powhatan, who accompanied Pocahontas, was directed in this manner to mark the number of the people he might meet. He obtained a very long cane on his landing, and commenced the task. But he soon became weary of this manner of taking the census, and, on his return home, said to his king, "Count the stars in the sky, the leaves on the trees, the sands on the seashore, but not the people of England."

Stanza l., line 9.

And then her arm unclasps, and she is of the dead.

Early in the year 1617, while preparing to return to her native land, she was taken sick, and died at the age of twenty-two. She was buried at Gravesend. Her firmness and resignation proved the sincerity of her piety; and, as Bancroft eloquently observes, "She was saved, as if by the hand of mercy, from beholding the extermination of the tribes from which she sprang, leaving a spotless name, and dwelling in memory under the form of perpetual youth."

WIDOW AT HER DAUGHTER'S BRIDAL.

Deal gently thou, whose hand hath won
  The young bird from its nest away,
Where careless, 'neath a vernal sun,
  She gayly caroll'd, day by day;
The haunt is lone, the heart must grieve,
  From whence her timid wing doth soar,
They pensive list at hush of eve,
  Yet hear her gushing song no more.

Deal gently with her; thou art dear,
  Beyond what vestal lips have told,
And, like a lamb from fountains clear,
  She turns confiding to thy fold;
She, round thy sweet domestic bower
  The wreath of changeless love shall twine,
Watch for thy step at vesper hour,
  And blend her holiest prayer with thine.

Deal gently thou, when, far away,
  Mid stranger scenes her foot shall rove,
Nor let thy tender care decay—
  (The soul of woman lives in love:)
And shouldst thou, wondering, mark a tear,
  Unconscious, from her eyelids break,
Be pitiful, and sooth the fear
  That man's strong heart may ne'er partake.

A mother yields her gem to thee,
  On thy true breast to sparkle rare,
She places 'neath thy household tree
  The idol of her fondest care,
And by thy trust to be forgiven,
  When judgment wakes in terror wild,
By all thy treasured hopes of heaven,
  Deal gently with the widow's child.

THE SUN.

Eye of thy Maker, which hath never slept
Since the Eternal Voice from chaos said
"*Let there be light!*" great monarch of the day,
How shall our dark, cold strain, fit welcome speak,
Fit praise? Lo! the poor pagan, kneeling, views
Thy burning chariot, to the highest sky
Roll on resistless, and with awe exclaims,
"The god! The god!" And shall we blame his creed,
For whom no heaven hath open'd, to reveal
A better faith? Where else could he descry
Such image of the Deity? such power
With goodness blending? From the reedy grass,
Wiry and sparse, that in the marshes springs,
To the most tremulous and tender shoot
Of the mimosa, from the shrinking bud
Nursed in the greenhouse, to the gnarled oak
Notching a thousand winters on its trunk,
All are the children of thy love, oh sun!
And by thy smile sustain'd.

Unresting orb!
Pursuest thou, mid the labyrinth of suns,
Some pathway of thine own? Say, dost thou sweep,
With all thy marshall'd planets in thy train,
In grand procession on, through boundless space,
Age after age, towards some mysterious point
Mark'd by His finger, who doth write thy date,
Thy "mene—mene—tekel," on the walls

Of the blue vault that spans our universe?
—But Thou, who rul'st the sun, the astonish'd soul
Shrinks as it takes Thy name. Almost it fears
To be forgotten, mid the myriad worlds
Which thou hast made.
And yet the sickliest leaf
That drinks thy dew reproves our unbelief.
The frail field-lily, which no florist's eye
Regards, doth win a glorious garniture,
To kings denied. So, while to dust we bow,
Needy and poor, oh! bid us learn the lore
Graved on the humblest lily's leaf, as deep
As on yon disk of fire—*to trust in Thee.*

THE EARLY BLUE-BIRD.

Blue-bird! on yon leafless tree,
Dost thou carol thus to me,
"Spring is coming! Spring is here?"
Say'st thou so, my birdie dear?
What is that, in misty shroud,
Stealing from the darken'd cloud?
Lo! the snow-flakes' gathering mound
Settles o'er the whiten'd ground,
Yet thou singest, blithe and clear,
"Spring is coming! Spring is here!"

Strik'st thou not too bold a strain?
Winds are piping o'er the plain;
Clouds are sweeping o'er the sky
With a black and threatening eye;
Urchins, by the frozen rill,
Wrap their mantles closer still;
Yon poor man, with doublet old,
Doth he shiver at the cold?
Hath he not a nose of blue?
Tell me, birdling, tell me true.

Spring's a maid of mirth and glee,
Rosy wreaths, and revelry:
Hast thou woo'd some winged love
To a nest in verdant grove?

Sung to her of greenwood bower,
Sunny skies that never lower?
Lured her with thy promise fair
Of a lot that knows no care?
Prythee, bird, in coat of blue,
Though a lover, tell her true.

Ask her if, when storms are long,
She can sing a cheerful song?
When the rude winds rock the tree,
If she'll closer cling to thee?
Then the blasts that sweep the sky,
Unappall'd shall pass thee by;
Though thy curtain'd chamber show
Siftings of untimely snow,
Warm and glad thy heart shall be,
Love shall make it Spring for thee.

THE ANCIENT MONUMENT.

THERE'S a lion under thy feet, Sir Knight,
And over thy head an escutcheon bright,
And group'd around, with mournful mien,
Kneeling kindred and friends are seen :
From some, old Time hath cloven the head,
Or the arm of marble away hath shred,
But thou, in thy perfect state art there,
With cuirass buckled, and forehead bare,
And pale hands lifted and clasp'd in prayer.

Where were the fields of thy proud career?
What were the deeds of thy glittering spear?
With thy good war-steed and thy helmed head,
Didst thou trample on heaps of the quivering dead?
Was thy banner on Syrian plains display'd?
Did it flame in the van of the red crusade?
Didst thou quaff thy cup of foaming wine,
And boldly lead the embattled line
To the leaguer'd gates of Palestine?

What was the price of thy warrior fame?
What was the cost of thy mighty name?
Did innocent blood profusely spilt
Tinge thy coat of mail with the hue of guilt?
Stern wert thou to thy vassal train?
Dead to the moaning of want and pain?

Lo ! the dust of the peasant is sleeping free
'Neath the holy shade of the church-yard tree :
Baron bold ! is it well with thee ?

I see on the scroll by thy couch of sleep,
The name of the Saviour engraven deep :
Was that thy chart when the sunbeam smiled ?
Was that thine anchor when storms were wild ?
When the shaft of the Spoiler had pierced thy heart,
Did it win the grief from that poison-dart ?
Then, till the dawn of the day of doom,
Till the trump of the angel shall break the gloom,
Rest in the peace of the Christian's tomb.

WINTER'S FÊTE.

I woke, and every lordling of the grove
Was clad in diamonds, and the lowliest shrub
Did wear its crest of brilliants gallantly.
The swelling hillocks, with their woven vines,
The far-seen forests, and the broken hedge,
Yea, every thicket gleam'd in bright array,
As for some gorgeous fête of fairy-land.

—Ho! jewel-keeper of the hoary North,
Whence hast thou all these treasures? Why, the mines
Of rich Golconda, since the world was young,
Would fail to furnish such a glorious show.
The queen, who to her coronation comes,
With half a realm's exchequer on her head,
Dazzleth the shouting crowd. But all the queens
Who since old Egypt's buried dynasty
Have here and there, amid the mists of time,
Lifted their tiny sceptres—all the throng
Of peeresses, who at some birth-night shine,
Might boast no moiety of the gems thy hand
So lavishly hath strewn o'er this old tree,
Fast by my window.

Every noteless thorn,
Even the coarse sumach and the bramble bush,
Do sport their diadems, as if, forsooth,
Our plain republic in a single night
Put forth such growth of aristocracy
That no plebeian in the land was left

Uncoroneted. Broider'd frost-work wraps
Yon stunted pear-tree, whose ne'er ripen'd fruit,
Acid and bitter, every truant-boy
Blamed with set teeth. Lo! while I speak, its crown
Kindleth in bossy crimson, and a stream
Of Tyrian purple, blent with emerald spark,
Floats round its rugged arms; while here and there
Gleams out a living sapphire, mid a knot
Of trembling rubies, whose exquisite ray
O'erpowers the astonish'd sight.
One arctic queen,
For one ice-palace, rear'd with fearful toil,
And soon dissolving, scrupled not to pay
Her vassal's life; and emperors of old
Have drain'd their coffers for the people's gaze,
Though but a single amphitheatre
Compress'd the crowd. But thou, whose potent wand
Call'd forth such grand enchantment, swift as thought,
And silent as a vision, and canst spread
Its wondrous beauty to each gazing eye,
Nor be the poorer, thou art scorn'd and bann'd
Mid all thy beauty. Summer scantly sheds
A few brief dew-drops for the sun to dry,
And wins loud praise from every piping swain
For the proud fête.
Yet, certes, in these days,
When wealth is so esteem'd that he who boasts
The longest purse is sure the wisest man,
Winter, who thus affords to sprinkle gems,
Mile after mile, on all the landscape round,
And decks his new-made peers in richer robes
Than monarch ever gave, deserves more thanks

Than to be call'd rude churl and miser old.
—I tell thee he's a friend, and Love, who sits
So quiet in the corner, whispering long
In beauty's ear, by the bright evening fire,
Shall join my verdict. Yes, the King of Storms,
So long decried, hath revenue more rich
Than sparkling diamonds.

Look within thy heart,
When the poor shiver in their snow-wreath'd cell,
Or the sad orphan mourns, and if thou find
An answering pity, and a fervent deed
Done in Christ's name, doubt not to be an heir
Of that true wealth, which Winter hoardeth up
To buy the soul a mansion with the blest.

NATIVE SCENERY.

Sweetly wild! sweetly wild!
Were the scenes that charm'd me when a child.
Rocks, gray rocks, with their tracery dark,
Leaping rills, like the diamond spark,
Torrent voices, thundering by,
When the pride of the vernal floods swell'd high;
And quiet roofs, like the hanging nest,
Mid cliffs by the feathery foliage dress'd.

—Beyond, in these woods, did the wild rose grow,
And the lily gleam white, where the lakelets flow,
And the trailing arbutus shroud its grace,
Till fragrance bewrayed its hiding-place,
And the woodbine hold to the dews its cup,
And the vine, with its clustering grapes, go up,
Up to the crest of the tallest trees;
And so, mid the humming-birds and bees,
On a seat of turf, embroidered fair
With the violet blue and the columbine rare,
It was sweet to sit, till the sun laid down,
At the gate of the west, his golden crown:
Sweetly wild! sweetly wild!
Were the scenes that charm'd me when a child.

DEATH OF AN INFANT IN ITS MOTHER'S ARMS.

"He slumbers long, young mother,
  Upon thy gentle breast;
Thou'rt weary now with watching,
  Sweet mother, go to rest:
There seems no pain to stir him,
  His peril sure is past,
For see, his soft hand clasp'd in thine,
  He heeds nor storm nor blast.

Why dost thou gaze so wildly?
  Why strain thy strong embrace?
Unlock thy fearful clasping,
  And let me see his face:"
So down that mother laid him,
  In her agony of care,
And kiss'd the cold and marble brow
  With calm and fix'd despair.

"Oh weep! there's holy healing
  In every gushing tear,
Nor question thus that beauteous clay,
  The angel is not here;

No shut of rose at eventide
  Was with a peace so deep,
As o'er thy darling's closing eye
  Stole his last dovelike sleep."

Where best he loved to hide him,
  In that dear sheltering spot,
Just there his tender spirit pass'd—
  Pass'd, and she knew it not:
His fond lip never trembled,
  Nor sigh'd the parting breath,
When strangely for his nectar'd draught
  He drank the cup of death.

Full was thy lot of blessing,
  To charm his cradle-hours,
To touch his sparkling fount of thought,
  And breathe his breath of flowers,
And take thy daily lesson
  From the smile that beam'd so free,
Of what in holier, brighter realms,
  The pure in heart must be.

No more thy twilight musing
  May with his image shine,
When in that lonely hour of love
  He laid his cheek to thine;
So still and so confiding
  That cherish'd babe would be,
So like a sinless guest from heaven,
  And yet a part of thee.

But now his blessed portion
  Is o'er the cloud to soar,
And spread a never-wearied wing
  Where sorrows are no more;
With cherubim and seraphim
  To tread the ethereal plain,
High honour hath it been to thee
  To swell that glorious train.

BREAD IN THE WILDERNESS.

A VOICE amid the desert.
                                        Not of him
Who, in rough garments clad, and locust-fed,
Cried to the sinful multitude, and claim'd
Fruits of repentance, with the lifted scourge
Of terror and reproof. A milder guide,
With gentler tones, doth teach the listening throng.
Benignant pity moved him as he saw
The shepherdless and poor. He knew to touch
The springs of every nature. The high lore
Of Heaven he humbled to the simplest child,
And in the guise of parable allured
The sluggish mind to follow truth and live.

They whom the thunders of the law had stunn'd
Woke to the Gospel's melody with tears;
And the glad Jewish mother held her babe
High in her arms, that its young eye might greet
Jesus of Nazareth.
                                        It was so still,
Though thousands cluster'd there, that not a sound
Brake the strong spell of eloquence which held
The wilderness in chains, save now and then,
As the gale freshen'd, came the murmur'd speech
Of distant billows, chafing with the shores
Of the Tiberian Sea.

Day wore apace,
Noon hasted, and the lengthening shadows brought
The unexpected eve. They linger'd still,
Eyes fix'd, and lips apart; the very breath
Constrain'd, lest some escaping sigh might break
The tide of knowledge, sweeping o'er their souls
Like a strange, raptured dream. They heeded not
The spent sun, closing at the curtain'd west
His burning journey. What was time to them,
Who heard entranced the eternal Word of Life?

But the weak flesh grew weary. Hunger came,
Sharpening each feature, and to faintness drain'd
Life's vigorous fount. The holy Saviour felt
Compassion for them. His disciples press,
Care-stricken, to his side: "Where shall we find
Bread in this desert?"
Then, with lifted eye,
He bless'd, and brake, the slender store of food,
And fed the famish'd thousands. Wondering awe
With renovated strength inspired their souls,
As, gazing on the miracle, they mark'd
The gather'd fragments of their feast, and heard
Such heavenly words as lip of mortal man
Had never utter'd.
Thou, whose pitying heart
Yearn'd o'er the countless miseries of those
Whom thou didst die to save, touch thou our souls
With the same spirit of untiring love.
Divine Redeemer! may our fellow-man,
Howe'er by rank or circumstance disjoin'd,
Be as a brother in his hour of need.

MIGRATION OF BIRDS.

November came on, with an eye severe,
And his stormy language was hoarse to hear;
And the glittering garland of brown and red,
Which he wreathed for a while round the forest's head,
With a sudden anger he rent away,
And all was cheerless, and bare, and gray.

Then the houseless grasshopper told his woes,
And the humming-bird sent forth a wail for the rose,
And the spider, that weaver of cunning so deep,
Roll'd himself up in a ball to sleep;
And the cricket his merry horn laid by
On the shelf, with the pipe of the dragon-fly.

Soon the birds were heard, at the morning prime,
Consulting of flight to a warmer clime.
"Let us go! let us go!" said the bright-wing'd jay;
And his gay spouse sang from a rocking spray,
"I am tired to death of this hum-drum tree,
I'll go, if 'tis only the world to see."

"Will you go?" asked the robin, "my only love?"
And a tender strain from the leafless grove
Responded, "Wherever your lot is cast,
Mid summer skies or the northern blast,
I am still at your side your heart to cheer,
Though dear is our nest in the thicket here."

"I am ready to go," cried the querulous wren,
"From the hateful homes of these northern men;
My throat is sore, and my feet are blue;
I fear I have caught the consumption too."
And the oriole told, with a flashing eye,
How his plumage was spoil'd by this frosty sky.

Then up went the thrush with a trumpet-call,
And the martins came forth from their box on the wall,
And the owlets peep'd out from their secret bower,
And the swallows convened on the old church-tower,
And the council of blackbirds was long and loud,
Chattering and flying from tree to cloud.

"The dahlia is dead on her throne," said they;
"And we saw the butterfly cold as clay;
Not a berry is found on the russet plains,
Not a kernel of ripen'd maize remains;
Every worm is hid—shall we longer stay
To be wasted with famine? Away! Away!"

But what a strange clamour on elm and oak,
From a bevy of brown-coated mocking-birds' broke;
The theme of each separate speaker they told
In a shrill report, with such mimicry bold,
That the eloquent orators started to hear
Their own true echo, so wild and clear.

Then tribe after tribe, with its leader fair,
Swept off, through the fathomless depths of air.
Who marketh their course to the tropics bright?
Who nerveth their wing for its weary flight?

Who guideth that caravan's trackless way
By the star at night and the cloud by day?

Some spread o'er the waters a daring wing,
In the isles of the southern sea to sing,
Or where the minaret, towering high,
Pierces the blue of the Moslem sky,
Or amid the harem's haunts of fear
Their lodges to build and their nurslings rear.

The Indian fig, with its arching screen,
Welcomes them in to its vistas green,
And the breathing buds of the spicy tree
Thrill at the burst of their melody,
And the bulbul starts, mid his carol clear,
Such a rushing of stranger-wings to hear.

O wild-wood wanderers! how far away
From your rural homes in our vales ye stray.
But when they are waked by the touch of Spring,
Shall we see you again with your glancing wing?
Your nests mid our household trees to raise,
And stir our hearts in our Maker's praise?

"SHOW US THE FATHER."

JOHN, iv., 8.

HAVE ye not *seen* Him, when through parted snows
Wake the first kindlings of the vernal green?
When 'neath its modest veil the arbutus blows,
And the pure snow-drop bursts its folded screen?
When the wild rose, that asks no florist's care,
Unfoldeth its rich leaves, have ye not seen Him there?

Have ye not *seen* Him, when the infant's eye,
Through its bright sapphire-windows shows the mind?
When, in the trembling of the tear or sigh,
Floats forth that essence, trembling and refined?
Saw ye not Him, the author of our trust,
Who breathed the breath of life into a frame of dust?

Have ye not *heard* Him, when the tuneful rill
Casts off its icy chains and leaps away?
In thunders echoing loud from hill to hill?
In songs of birds, at break of summer's day?
Or in the ocean's everlasting roar,
Battling the old gray rocks that sternly guard his shore?

Amid the stillness of the Sabbath morn,
When vexing cares in tranquil slumber rest,
When in the heart the holy thought is born,
And Heaven's high impulse warms the waiting breast,

Have ye not *felt* Him, while your kindling prayer
Swelled out in tones of praise, announcing God was there?

Show us the Father! If ye fail to trace
His chariot where the stars majestic roll,
His pencil mid earth's loveliness and grace,
His presence in the sabbath of the soul,
How can you see Him till the day of dread,
When to assembled worlds the book of doom is read?

THE RAINY DAY.

When the soft summer-shower, whose herald-drops
Stirr'd the broad vine-leaves to an answering joy,
Swells to protracted rain, soothing the mind
With sense of leisure, mother, haste to call
Thy little flock around thee. Let them hail
The rainy day, as one when tender love
Brings forth for them its richest stores of thought.
Think'st thou the needle's thrift or housewife's lore
Yields richer payment? Mother! thou mayst stamp
Such trace upon the waxen mind as life,
With all its swelling floods, shall ne'er blot out.
So take thy bright-eyed nursling on thy knee,
And tell him of the God who rules the cloud
And calms the tempest, and the glorious sun
Brings forth rejoicing from the rosy east
To gild the morn.
Unlock thy treasured hoards
Of hallow'd lore: how little Samuel heard
At midnight, 'neath the temple's solemn arch,
Jehovah's voice, and hasted to obey:
How young Josiah turned to Israel's God
Ere yet eight summers ripen'd on his brow:
And how the sick child to his father cried,
"My head! my head!" then, in his mother's arms,
Grew pale and died: and how the prophet's prayer
Did pluck him from the jaws of death again.

F

Tell, too, thy little daughter, while she sits
Heedful beside thee, how the shepherds heard
The harps of angels while they watch'd their sheep:
And how the infant Saviour found no bed
Save a straw manger mid the horned train:
And how he raised the ruler's daughter up,
When on her dead brow lay the weeper's tear:
How at the tomb of Lazarus he mourn'd
With the sad sisters: and, when the wild sea,
And wilder tempest raged, stretch'd out his hand
And saved the faint disciple on the wave,
Who pray'd to him.
Then, when the moisten'd eye
Reveals the softening soul, cast in thy seed,
And Heaven and holy angels water it!
So shall the spirit of the summer-storm
Gleam as a rainbow, when thy soul goes up,
With its dread company of deeds and thoughts,
To bide the audit of the day of doom.

AFRAID TO DIE.

"And deliver them who, through fear of death, were all their lifetime subject to bondage."—*Hebrews*, ii., 15.

Afraid to die!—afraid to sleep
  In earth, our mother's tranquil breast,
Where snares and troubles vex no more,
  And all the weary are at rest?

Afraid to die!—afraid to take
  His hand who trod the shadowy vale,
And leads us on to pastures green,
  And living streams that never fail?

Afraid to die!—afraid to bear
  The pang that but a moment tries,
And, o'er the sway of pain and care,
  Ascend to mansions in the skies?

Afraid to die!—afraid to leave
  The cradle and the worthless toy,
And take our ripen'd being's crown,
  And soar to consummated joy?

Afraid to die!—afraid to trust
  His promise who shall burst the tomb,
And raise the renovated dust
  More glorious from its transient gloom?

Afraid to die !—afraid to meet
  The guardian bands who watchful wait,
And spread their radiant pinions wide
  To bear us through salvation's gate ?

Afraid to die !—prefer to be
  A stranger in these courts below,
A pilgrim, when the lights of home
  Bright through our Father's windows glow ?

Afraid to die !—ah ! what avails,
  Whether by sickness, storm, or fire ;
The ethereal essence finds its place,
  And rises to the Eternal Sire ?

Afraid to die ?—O grant us grace,
  Thou who didst dare the spoiler's strife,
Calmly to meet his cold embrace,
  And soar to everlasting life.

THE BEREAVED.

"Not my will, but thine."

I HAD a little blossom, its nursing-root was dead,
And in my breast I hid it when its angel mother fled,
But at every blast I shudder'd, and I trembled day and night,
Lest some unseen destroyer my only bud should blight.

Two years of anxious care, yet of high and sacred joy,
Brought forth, in ruddy health, my lovely, blooming boy,
With the curls around his head, and the lustre in his eye,
And the music on his lip, like a song-bird of the sky.

In wakeful hours I mused, and I wish'd, while others sleep,
That, for his precious sake, my wealth was broad and deep;
So I forced my lingering mind for a little while to go
And gather for my son, where the gold and silver grow.

The old nurse loved my blooming boy, and round her neck
he clung
With his clasping, ivory arms, and his busy, flattering
tongue;
She promised to be faithful, with the tear upon her cheek,
And I tore myself away as he lay in slumbers meek.

Both night and day I toil'd, while my heart was with the
child,
And on my every labour propitious Fortune smiled;

Then I homeward set my face, when the spring-flowers
'gan to blow—
O for an eagle's pinion! the flying car, how slow.

I brought the baubles that he loved, the tiny gilded drum,
The crimson-banner'd host, that to mimic battle come,
The Argonautic shells, that sail in pearly fleet,
And, in its pretty cage, the bright-winged paroquet.

My trees! my roof! I knew them well, though midnight's
veil was drear,
The pale nurse-lamp was flickering within the nursery dear,
But a muffled watcher started thence at my impatient tread,
And there my darling lay, on his white mattress-bed.

How still! My God, is there no voice? And has it come
to this!
The white lip quivereth not to my impassion'd kiss!
'Tis a coldness like the grave! My idol! can it be?
O Father, from thy throne above, in mercy look on me.

They told me how the fever raged, and, in his broken dream,
How he call'd upon the absent, with shrill and frantic scream,
How he set his teeth on cup and spoon, with hated medi-
cine fraught,
But at his father's treasured name, he took the bitterest
draught.

God gave me strength to make his bed where his young
mother slept,
The fragrant vines she used to train around her feet had
crept,

But I cut their roots away, that the bud she loved the best
Might spread its wither'd petals upon her pulseless breast.

And now I wander wide beneath a foreign sky,
In the stranger's home I lodge, for no household hearth
have I,
There are gray hairs on my temples, despite my early
years,
But I find there's still a comfort in drying others' tears.

Why should I cloud my brow? why yield to dark despair?
All—all men are my brethren, and this fruitful earth is fair,
For I know, when heaven hath wounded and probed the
bleeding breast,
Its richest, healing balm is, in making others bless'd.

The poor man he doth thank me, and the orphan's grateful
prayer
Breathes sweetly o'er my lonely soul, and sooths away
its care;
In the sick peasant's cabin the gift he needs I lay,
And, ere he knows the giver, I vanish far away.

I have a sacred joy, close lock'd from mortal eye,
My loved ones come to visit me when lost in dreams I lie;
They speak such words to charm me as only angels say,
And the beauty of their robes of light gleams round me
through the day.

God is their keeper, and their friend, their bliss no tongue
can tell,
And more I love His holy name that in His home they dwell;

O may He grant me grace divine, while on these shores of time,
To learn the dialect they speak in yon celestial clime.

Beside his glorious throne they rest, on seraph-harps they play;
Why should I wish them back again in these cold tents of clay?
A stricken, not a mournful man, I sigh, but not repine,
For my heart is in that land of love, with those I hope to join.

THE POET'S BOOKS.

A Poet should be conversant with God
In all his works. For, from the untrodden cliff
Where fiery Andes mocks the driven cloud,
To the obscurest moss which arctic storms
Deny an efflorescence, from the roar
Of the wild rainbow-cinctured cataract,
To the slight ripple of the loneliest lake,
All speak of Him.
Choose not the ponderous tomes
Where Science wastes away the oil of life,
And early hoary, seeks the voiceless tomb,
Its lessons still unlearn'd; nor lose thyself
In the entangling lore of many lands,
Until thy mother tongue seem strange to thee.
Much knowledge is much toil, and hath no end.
But come thou forth, amid the breeze-swept trees,
And learn their language. Ask the peaceful vales,
Where roam the herds, or where the reaper plies
His busy sickle—ask the solemn sea,
With all its foaming wilderness of waves,
To spread its mighty volume out for thee,
And search thou there, on every fearful page,
Jehovah's name.
Question the rough-leafed herb,
That lines the simpler's scrip, nor scorn to heed
Such answer as its healing essence yields.

Talk with the firefly when it gilds the eve,
And catch the murmur of the waving boughs,
Where hides the slumbering nest.

List, when old night,
That dark-robed queen, disbands the muffled stars,
And boldly writeth on the vaulted sky
Its Maker's awful name. When weary day,
Casting her deeds into gray twilight's lap,
Doth sleep, forgetful of the Judge, be there,
A student of its annal, if perchance
Its varying burden, fitted to thy harp,
May yield true wisdom.

Take thy choicest books
From Nature's library, and be thy creed
Such soul-entrancing poesy as makes
Virtue more lovely, and inspires the hymn
That seraphs set to music.

OAK IN AUTUMN.

Old oak! old oak! the chosen one,
  Round which my poet's mesh I twine,
When rosy wakes the joyous sun,
  Or, wearied, sinks at day's decline,
I see the frost-king here and there,
  Claim some brown leaflet for his own,
Or point in cold derision where
  He soon shall rear the usurper's throne.

Too soon! too soon! in crimson bright,
  Vain mockery of thy wo, he'll flout,
And proudly climb thy topmost height,
  To hang his flaunting signal out;
While thou, as round thine honours fall,
  Shalt stand with seam'd and naked bark,
Like banner-staff, so lone and tall,
  His ruthless victory to mark.

I, too, old friend, when thou art gone,
  Must pensive to my casement go,
Or, like the shuddering Druid, moan
  The withering of his mistletoe;
But when young Spring, with matin clear,
  Awakes the bird, the stream, the tree,
Fain would I at her call appear,
  And hang my slender wreath on thee.

LOVE NOT THE WORLD.

To gain the friendship of the world,
How vain the ceaseless strife;
We sow the sand, we grasp the wind,
We waste the life of life.

Perchance some giddy height we gain,
Some gilded treasure show,
The footing fails, the shadow 'scapes,
We sink in deeper wo.

Yet, baffled, still the toil we try,
The eager chase renew,
Even though the portals of the grave
Yawn on our startled view.

But Thou, whose pitying mercy's tide
Is like the unfathom'd sea,
Thy love was waiting for our souls,
That would not turn to Thee;

Thy hand was stretch'd, Thy voice was heard,
Thy fold was open wide,
Ah! who the straying sheep can save
That shuns the Eternal Guide?

VISIT TO THE BIRTHPLACE.

Bright summer's flush was on thee, clime beloved,
When last I trod thy vales. Now, all around,
Autumn her rainbow energy of tint
Poureth o'er copse and forest, beautiful,
Yet speaking of decay. The aspiring pine
Wears his undying green; but the strong oak,
Like smitten giant, casts his honours down,
Strewing brown earth with emerald and gold.
Yon lofty elms, the glory of our land,
So lately drooping 'neath their weight of leaves,
With proud, yet graceful elegance, to earth,
Stand half in nakedness, and half in show
Of gaudy colours. Hath some secret shaft
Wounded the maple's breast, that thus it bends
Like bleeding warrior, tinging all its robes
With crimson? while in pity by its side,
The pallid poplar, turning to the eye
Its silver lining, moans at every breeze.

I roved in sadness through those alter'd scenes.
The voice of man was painful. On the ear
Idly and vague it fell, for tearful thought
Wrought inward, mid the faded imagery
Of early days.
See there, yon low-brow'd cot,
Whose threshold oft my childish foot has cross'd

So merrily, whose hearth-stone shone so bright
At eve, where with her skilful needle wrought
The industrious matron, while our younger group
Beguiled with fruit, and nuts, and storied page
The winter's stormy hour: where is she now?
Who coldly answers? *dead!*
Fast by its side
A dearer mansion stands, where my young eyes
First open'd on the light. That garden's bound,
Where erst I roam'd delighted, deeming earth,
With all its wealth, had naught so beautiful
As its trim hedge of roses, and the ranks
Of daffodils, with snowdrops at their feet,
How small and changed it seems! The velvet turf,
With its cool arbour, where I linger'd long
Conning my little lesson, or, perchance,
Eying the slowly-ripening peach, that lean'd
Its downy cheek against the latticed wall,
Or holding converse with the violet-buds,
That were to me as sisters, giving back
Sweet thoughts: say, is it not less green than when
My childhood wander'd there?
Lo! by rude rocks
O'ercanopied, the dome where science taught
Her infant rudiments. First day of school!
I well remember thee, just on the verge
Of my fourth summer. Every face around
How wonderful and new! The months moved on
Majestically slow. Awe-struck, I mark'd
The solemn schooldame in her chair of state,
Much fearing lest her all-observant eye
Might note me wandering from my patchwork task

Or spelling lesson. Yet that frigid realm
Some sunbeams boasted, whose delicious warmth
Lent nutriment to young ambition's germes.
"Head of the class!" what music in that sound,
Link'd to my name; and then, the crowning joy,
Homeward to bear, on shoulder neatly pinn'd,
The bow of crimson satin, rich reward
Of well-deserving, not too lightly won
Or worn too meekly. Still ye need not scorn
Our humble training, ye of modern times,
Wiser and more accomplish'd. Learning's field,
Indeed, was circumscribed, but its few plants
Had such close pruning and strict discipline
As giveth healthful root and hardy stalk,
Perchance, enduring fruit.
Beneath yon roof—
Our own no more—beneath my planted trees,
Where unfamiliar faces now appear,
She dwelt, whose hallow'd welcome was so dear;
O Mother, Mother! all thy priceless love
Is fresh before me, as of yesterday.
Thy pleasant smile, the beauty of thy brow,
Thine idol fondness for thine only one,
The untold tenderness with which thy heart
Embraced my firstborn infant, when my joys,
Swelling to their full climax, bore it on,
With its young look of wonder, to thy home,
A stranger visitant. Fade, visions, fade!
Ye make her vacant place too visible,
Ye stir the sources of the bitter tear,
When I would think of her eternal gain,
And praise my God for her.

And now farewell,
Dear native spot! with fairest landscapes deck'd,
Of old romantic cliff, and crystal rill,
And verdant soil, enrich'd with proudest wealth,
Warm hearts and true.
Yet deem not I shall wear
The mourner's weeds for thee. Another home
Hath joys and duties. And, where'er my path
On earth shall lead, I'll keep a nesting bough
For hope, the song-bird, and, with cheerful step,
Hold on my pilgrimage, remembering where
Flowers have no autumn-languor, Eden's gate
No flaming sword, to guard the tree of life.

FUNERAL OF A NEIGHBOUR.

Ah! can that funeral knell be thine,
  Thou, at whose image kind
So many long-remember'd scenes
  Come rushing o'er my mind?
Thy rural home behind the trees,
  Thy bowers with roses dress'd,
And the bright eye and beaming smile,
  That cheer'd each entering guest.

There, when our children, hand in hand,
  Pursued their earnest play,
It drew our hearts more closely still,
  To see their own so gay,
And hear their merry laughter ring
  Around the evening hearth,
While the loud threat of winter's storm
  Broke not their hour of mirth.

'Tis strange that I should seek in vain
  That mansion, once so fair,
And find the spot where erst it stood
  All desolate and bare;
Its smooth green bank, on which so thick
  The dappled daisies grew—
How passing strange, that from its place
  Even that has vanish'd too.

But thou, whatever change or cloud
  Deform'd this lower sky,
Hadst still a fountain in thy heart
  Whose streams were never dry;
A fountain of perennial hope,
  That never ceased to flow,
And give its sky-fed crystals forth
  To every child of wo.

Thy frequent visits to my couch,
  If sickness paled my cheek,
And all thy sympathetic love,
  Which language cannot speak,
How strong those recollections rise
  To wake the grateful tear,
For deeds like these more precious grow
  With every waning year.

I cannot think that bitter grief
  Would please thy happy soul,
Raised as thou art to that bless'd world
  Where tempests never roll;
But may thy dearest and thy best,
  The children of thy care,
Walk steadfast in thy chosen path,
  And joyful meet thee there.

THE AGED BISHOP.

A scene at the closing of a Convention in Virginia, by the venerable Bishop Moore.

THEY cluster'd round, that listening throng,
The parting hour drew nigh,
And heighten'd feeling, deep and strong,
Spoke forth from eye to eye;

For reverend in his hoary years,
A white-robed prelate bent,
And trembling pathos wing'd his words,
As to the heart they went.

With saintly love he urged the crowd
Salvation's hope to gain,
While, gathering o'er his furrow'd cheek,
The tears fell down like rain;

He waved his hand, and music woke
A warm and solemn strain,
His favourite hymn swell'd high, and fill'd
The consecrated fane.

Then from the hallow'd chancel forth,
With faltering step, he sped,
And fervent laid a father's hand
On every priestly head,

And breathed the blessing of his God.
And, full of meekness, said,
"Be faithful in your Master's work
When your old bishop's dead.

"For more than fifty years, my sons,
A Saviour's love supreme
Unto a sinful world, hath been
My unexhausted theme;

"Now, see, the blossoms of the grave
Are o'er my temples spread,
Oh! lead the seeking soul to Him
When your old bishop's dead."

Far waned the holy Sabbath-eve
On toward the midnight hour,
Before the spellbound throng retired
To slumber's soothing power;

Yet many a sleeper, mid his dream,
Beheld in snowy stole
That patriarch-prelate's bending form,
Whose accents stirr'd the soul.

In smiles the summer morn arose,
And many a grateful guest,
Forth from those hospitable domes,
With tender memories, press'd,

While o'er the broad and branching bay,
Which like a heart doth pour
A living tide, in countless streams,
Through fair Virginia's shore,

O'er Rappahannock's fringed breast,
O'er rich Potomac's tide,
Or where the bold, resistless James
Rolls on, with monarch-pride,

The boats that ask nor sail nor oar,
With speed majestic glide,
And many a thoughtful pastor leans
In silence o'er their side,

And, while he seems to scan the flood
In silver 'neath him spread,
Revolves the charge, "*Be strong for God*
When your old bishop's dead."

POWER OF THE ALMIGHTY.

God of the chainless winds, that wildly wreck
The moaning forest, and the ancient oak
Rend like a sapling spray, and sweep the sand
O'er the lost caravan, that trod, with pride
Of tinkling bells, and camel's arching neck,
The burning desert—a dense host at morn,
At eve a bubble on the trackless waste—
God of the winds! canst thou not rule the heart,
And gather back its passions when thou wilt,
Bidding them "*Peace: be still!*"
God of the waves,
That toss and mock the mightiest argosy,
As the wild zephyr frets the thistle-down,
Until the sternest leader's heart doth melt
Because of trouble—Thou who call'st them back
From their rough challenge to the muffled sky,
And bidd'st them harmless lave an infant's feet
That seeketh silver shells—canst Thou not curb
The tumult of the nations, the hot wrath
Of warring kings, who, like the babe, must die;
Vaunting this day in armour, and the next,
Unshrouded, slumbering on the battle-field?
God of the unfathom'd, unresisted deep!
We trust in Thee, and know in whom we trust.

—God of the solemn stars, that tread so true
The path by thee appointed, every one,

From the slight asteroid to the vast orb
That lists the watchword, or the music-march
Of farthest planets round their monarch suns,
Marshall'd in glorious ranks, so teach our souls,
That when, unbodied from this lower world,
Trembling, they launch, they may not lose the clew
That guides from sun to sun, through boundless space,
The stranger-atom to a home with Thee.

HOME OF THE DUELLIST.

The mother sat beside her fire,
Well trimm'd it was and bright,
While loudly moan'd the forest-pines
Amid that wintry night.

She heard them not, those wind-swept pines,
For o'er a scroll she hung,
That bore her husband's voice of love,
As when that love was young.

And thrice her son, beside her knee,
Besought her favouring eye,
And thrice her lisping daughter spoke,
Before she made reply.

"O, little daughter, many a kiss
Lies in this treasured line;
And, boy, a father's blessed prayers,
And counsels fond, are thine.

"Thou hast his high and arching brow,
Thou hast his eye of flame;
And be the purpose of thy soul,
Thy sun-bright course, the same."

And, as she drew them to her arms,
Down her fair cheek would glide

A gushing tear like diamond spark,
  A tear of love and pride.

She took her baby from its rest,
  And laid it on her knee:
"Thou ne'er hast seen thy sire," she said,
  "But he'll be proud of thee:

"Yes, he'll be proud of thee, my dove,
  The lily of our line,
I know what eye of blue he loves,
  And such an eye is thine."

"Where is my father gone, mamma?
  Why does he stay so long?"
"He's far away in Congress' Hall,
  Amid the noble throng:

"He's in the lofty Congress' Hall,
  To swell the high debate,
And help to frame those equal laws
  That make our land so great.

"But ere the earliest violets bloom
  We in his arms shall be,
So go to rest, my children dear,
  And pray for him and me."

The snow-flakes rear'd their drifted mound
  O'er hill and valley deep,
But nought amid that peaceful home
  Disturb'd the dews of sleep;

For lightly, like an angel's dream,
 The trance of slumber fell,
Where innocence and holy love
 Maintain'd their guardian spell.

Another eve—another scroll.
 Wist ye what words it said?
Two words, two awful words it bore,
 The duel! and the dead!

The duel? and the dead? How dim
 Was that young mother's eye,
How fearful was her lengthen'd swoon,
 How wild her piercing cry.

There's many a wife whose bosom's lord
 Is in his prime laid low,
Ingulf'd beneath the wat'ry main,
 Where bitter tempests blow;

Or crush'd amid the battle-field,
 Where slaughter'd thousands rest;
Yet know they of the speechless pang
 That rives her bleeding breast?

Who lies so powerless on her couch,
 Transfix'd by sorrow's sting?
Her infant in its nurse's arms,
 Like a forgotten thing.

A dark-hair'd boy is at her side—
 He lifts his eagle-eye:

"Mother! they say my father's dead;
  How did my father die?"

Again the spear-point in her breast!
  Again that shriek of pain!
"Child! thou hast riven thy mother's soul:
  Speak not those words again."

"Speak not those words again, my son!"
  What boots the fruitless care?
They're written wheresoe'er she turns,
  On ocean, earth, or air:

They're sear'd upon her shrinking heart,
  That bursts beneath its doom:
The duel! and the dead! they haunt
  The threshold of her tomb.

Yes, through her brief and weary years
  That broken heart she bore,
And on her desolated cheek
  The smile sat never more.

THE PILGRIM.

"I am not far from home, therefore I need not make much provision for the way."

I HEAR the rising tempest moan,
My failing limbs have weary grown;
The flowers are shut, the streams are dried,
The arid sands spread drear and wide,
The night dews fall, the winds are high,
How far from home, O Lord, am I?

I would not come with hoards of gold,
With glittering gems or cumbrous mould,
Nor dim my eyes with gather'd dust
Of empty fame or earthly trust,
But hourly ask, as lone I roam,
How far from home? how far from home?

Not far! not far! the way is dark,
Fair hope hath quench'd her glow-worm spark;
The trees are dead beneath whose shade
My youth reclined, my childhood play'd;
Red lightning streaks the troubled sky,
How far from home, my God, am I?

Oh, find me in that home a place
Beneath the footstool of thy grace;

Though sometimes mid the husks I fed,
And turn'd me from the children's bread,
Still bid thine angel-harps resound,
The dead doth live, the lost is found.

Reach forth thy hand with pitying care,
And guide me through the latest snare;
Methinks, even now, in bursting beams
The radiance from thy casement streams;
No more I shed the pilgrim tear;
I hear thy voice, my home is near.

THOUGHTS AMONG THE TREES.

"The retiring of the mind into itself is the state most susceptible of divine impressions."—LORD BACON.

How beautiful you are, green trees! green trees!
How nobly beautiful! Fain would I rest
'Neath the broad shadow of your mantling arms,
And lose the world's unquiet imagery
In the soft mist of dreams. Your curtaining veil
Shuts out the revelry and toil, that chafe
The city's denizens. Man wars with man,
And brethren forage on each other's hearts,
Throwing their life-blood in that crucible
Which brings forth gold.

Unceasingly we strive,
And gaze at gauds, and cling to wind-swept reeds,
Then darkly sink, and die.

But here ye stand,
Your moss-grown roots by hidden moisture fed,
And on your towering heads the dews that fall
From God's right hand. I love your sacred lore,
And to the silence you have learn'd of Him
Bow down my spirit. Not a whispering leaf
Uplifts itself, to mar the holy pause
Of meditation.

Doth not wisdom dwell
With silence and with nature? From the throng

Of fierce communings or of feverish joys,
So the sweet mother of the Lord of life
Turn'd to the manger and its lowly train,
And, mid their quiet ruminations, found
Refuge and room.
Methinks an angel's wing
Floats o'er your arch of verdure, glorious trees!
Luring the soul above. O, ere we part,
For soon I leave your blessed company,
And seek the dusky paths of life again,
Give me some gift, some token of your love,
One holy thought, in heavenly silence born,
That I may nurse it till we meet again.

FAREWELL TO A RURAL RESIDENCE.

How beautiful it stands,
  Behind its elm-tree's screen,
With simple attic cornice crown'd,
  All graceful and serene;
Most sweet, yet sad, it is
  Upon yon scene to gaze,
And list its inborn melody,
  The voice of other days;

For there, as many a year
  Its varied chart unroll'd,
I hid me in those quiet shades,
  And call'd the joys of old;
I call'd them, and they came
  When vernal buds appear'd,
Or where the vine-clad summer bower
  Its temple-roof uprear'd,

Or where the o'erarching grove
  Spread forth its copses green,
While eye-bright and asclepias rear'd
  Their untrain'd stalks between,
And the squirrel from the boughs
  His broken nuts let fall,
And the merry, merry little birds
  Sang at his festival.

Yon old forsaken nests
  Returning spring shall cheer,
And thence the unfledged robin breathe
  His greeting wild and clear;
And from yon clustering vine,
  That wreathes the casement round,
The humming-birds' unresting wing
  Send forth a whirring sound;

And where alternate springs
  The lilach's purple spire
Fast by its snowy sister's side;
  Or where, with wing of fire,
The kingly oriole glancing went
  Amid the foliage rare,
Shall many a group of children tread,
  But mine will not be there.

Fain would I know what forms
  The mastery here shall keep,
What mother in yon nursery fair
  Rock her young babes to sleep:
Yet blessings on the hallow'd spot,
  Though here no more I stray,
And blessings on the stranger-babes
  Who in those halls shall play.

Heaven bless you, too, my plants,
  And every parent bird
That here, among the woven boughs,
  Above its young hath stirr'd.

I kiss your trunks, ye ancient trees,
That often o'er my head
The blossoms of your flowery spring
In fragrant showers have shed.

Thou, too, of changeful mood,
I thank thee, sounding stream,
That blent thine echo with my thought,
Or woke my musing dream.
I kneel upon the verdant turf,
For sure my thanks are due
To moss-cup and to clover-leaf,
That gave me draughts of dew.

To each perennial flower,
Old tenants of the spot,
The broad-leaf'd lily of the vale,
And the meek forget-me-not,
To every daisy's dappled brow,
To every violet blue,
Thanks! thanks! may each returning year
Your changeless bloom renew.

Praise to our Father-God,
High praise, in solemn lay,
Alike for what his hand hath given,
And what it takes away:
And to some other loving heart
May all this beauty be
The dear retreat, the Eden-home
That it hath been to me.

FOLLY.

"The fool hath said in his heart, there is no God."
Psalm xiv.

"*No God! no God!*" The simplest flower
That on the wild is found,
Shrinks as it drinks its cup of dew,
And trembles at the sound.
"No God!" astonished echo cries
From out her cavern hoar,
And every wandering bird that flies
Reproves the atheist-lore.

The solemn forest lifts its head,
The Almighty to proclaim,
The brooklet, on its crystal urn,
Doth leap to grave his name:
High swells the deep and vengeful sea
Along his billowy track,
And red Vesuvius opes his mouth,
To hurl the falsehood back.

The palm-tree, with its princely crest,
The cocoa's leafy shade,
The bread-fruit, bending to its lord,
In yon far island-glade;
The winged seeds that, borne by winds,
The roving sparrows feed,
The melon on the desert-sands,
Confute the scorner's creed.

"*No God!*" With indignation high
  The fervent sun is stirr'd,
And the pale moon turns paler still
  At such an impious word;
And, from their burning thrones, the stars
  Look down with angry eye,
That thus a worm of dust should mock
  Eternal Majesty.

THE DEPARTED PASTOR.

You will not see him more. You whose young thoughts
Blent with his image, who to manhood grew
Beneath the shelter of his saintly shade,
Bringing your tender infants to his hand
For the baptismal water, and lived on
Amid his teachings, till the silver hairs
Came all unlook'd for, stealing o'er your brow,
You will not see him more.

There was a place
Where, duly as the day of God return'd,
His solemn voice held converse with the skies
For you and yours, till more than fourscore years
Swept in deep billows o'er him. You will hear
That voice no more.

There stands his ancient house,
Where, with the partner of his heart, he shared
Affection's joys so long, and fondly mark'd
His children and his children's children rise
Clustering around his board.

Remember ye
His cordial welcome? how he freely dealt
A patriarch's wisdom, in monitions kind
To all who sought him? how, with hallow'd grace
Of bounteous hospitality, he gave
Example of those virtues, pure and sweet,

Which, round the hearth-stone rooting, have their fruit
Where men are judged?

He linger'd with you late,
Till all the loved companions of his youth
Had gone to rest. Yet so he loved your souls,
That for their sakes he willingly sustain'd
Life's toil and cumbrance, and stood forth alone,
An aged oak, amid the fallen grove.

—His Master call'd.

It was the Sabbath morn:
And he had girded up his loins to speak
A message in the Temple. Time had strown
The almond-blossom, and his head was white
As snows of winter, yet his step was firm,
And in his heart the same unblenching zeal
That warm'd his youth.

But, lo! the Master call'd.
So, laying down the Bible that he loved,
That single weapon he so meek had borne
Through all life's tribulation, he gave back
The spirit to its Giver, and went home;
Yes, full of honours as of days, went home.

SACRED MUSIC.

The King of Israel sat in state
  Within his palace fair,
Where falling fountains, pure and cool,
  Assuaged the summer air;

But shrouded was the son of Kish,
  Mid all his royal grace;
The tempest of a troubled soul
  Swept flashing o'er his face.

In vain were pomp, or regal power,
  Or courtier's flattering tone,
For pride and hatred basely sat
  Upon his bosom's throne.

He call'd upon his minstrel-boy,
  With hair as bright as gold,
Reclining in a deep recess,
  Where droop'd the curtain's fold.

Upon his minstrel-boy he call'd,
  And forth the stripling came,
Bright beauty on his ruddy brow,
  Like morn's enkindling flame.

"Give music," said the moody king,
  Nor raised his gloomy eye:

"Thou son of Jesse, bring the harp,
And wake its melody."

He thought upon his father's flock,
Which long, in pastures green,
He led, while flow'd, with silver sound,
Clear rivulets between.

He thought of Bethlehem's star-lit skies,
Beneath whose liquid rays
He gazed upon the glorious arch,
And sang its Maker's praise.

Then boldly o'er the sacred harp
He pour'd, in thrilling strain,
The prompting of a joyous heart,
That knew nor care nor pain.

The monarch, leaning on his hand,
Drank long the wondrous lay,
And clouds were lifted from his brow,
As when the sunbeams play.

The purple o'er his heaving breast,
That throbb'd so wild, grew still,
And Saul's clear eye glanced out, as when
He did Jehovah's will.

O ye who feel the poison-fumes
Of earth's fermenting care
Steal o'er the sky of hope, and dim
What Heaven created fair,

Should languid piety decline
  Within your erring breast,
Or baleful passion's scorpion-sting
  Bereave your soul of rest,

Ask music from a guileless heart,
  High tones, with sweetness fraught,
And, by that alchymy divine,
  Subdue the sinful thought.

THE RUINS OF HEROD'S PALACE.

THE traveller sat upon a stone,
  A broken column's pride,
And o'er his head a fig-tree waved
  Its grateful umbrage wide,
While round him fruitful valleys smiled,
  And crystal streams ran by,
And the bold mountain's forehead hoar
  Rose up 'tween earth and sky.

But on a ruin'd pile he gazed,
  Beneath whose mouldering gloom
The roving fox a shelter found,
  And noisome bats a tomb.
"Ho, Arab!" for a ploughman wrought
  The grassy sward among,
With marble fragments richly strew'd,
  And terraced olives hung,

"Say, canst thou tell what ancient dome
  In darkness here declines,
And strangely lifts its spectral form
  Among the matted vines?"
He stay'd his simple plough, that traced
  Its crooked furrow nigh,
And, while his oxen cropp'd the turf,
  Look'd up with vacant eye.

"It was some satrap's palace, sure,
  In old time, far away,
Or else of some great Christian prince,
  I've heard my father say,"
"Arab! it was King Herod's dome;
  'Twas there he feasted, free,
His captains, and the chief estates,
  And lords of Galilee;

"'Twas there the impious dancer's heel
  Lured his rash soul astray."
But, ere the earnest tale was told,
  The ploughman turn'd away.
O ruthless king! thy vaunted pomp
  And power avail thee not,
Who here, beside thy palace-gates,
  Art by the serf forgot:

Yet he whose blood in prison-cell
  By thy decree was spilt,
Whose head, upon the charger brought,
  Appeased revengeful guilt,
His name, amid a deathless page,
  Gleams forth with living ray,
While all thy royalty and pride
  Are swept like foam away.

MONODY ON MRS. HEMANS.

Nature doth mourn for thee. There comes a voice
From her far solitudes, as though the winds
Murmured low dirges, or the waves complain'd.
Even the meek plant, that never sang before,
Save one brief requiem, when its blossoms fell,
Seems through its drooping leaves to sigh for thee,
As for a florist dead. The ivy wreathed
Round the gray turrets of a buried race,
And the proud palm-trees, that like princes rear
Their diadems 'neath Asia's sultry sky,
Blend with their ancient lore thy hallowed name.

Thy music, like baptismal dew, did make
Whate'er it touched more holy. The pure shell,
Pressing its pearly lip to ocean's floor,
The cloister'd chambers where the sea-gods sleep,
And the unfathom'd, melancholy main,
Lament for thee, through all the sounding deeps.

Hark! from sky-piercing Himmaleh, to where
Snowdon doth weave his coronet of cloud,
From the scath'd pine-tree near the red-man's hut,
To where the everlasting banian builds
Its vast columnar temple, comes a wail
For her who o'er the dim cathedral's arch,
The quivering sunbeam on the cottage wall,

Or the sere desert, pour'd the lofty chant
And ritual of the muse : who found the link
That joins mute nature to ethereal mind,
And made that link a melody.

The vales
Of glorious Albion heard thy tuneful fame,
And those green cliffs, where erst the Cambrian bards
Swept their indignant lyres, exulting tell
How oft thy fairy foot in childhood climb'd
Their rude, romantic heights. Yet was the couch
Of thy last slumber in yon verdant isle
Of song, and eloquence, and ardent soul,
Which, loved of lavish skies, though bann'd by fate,
Seem'd as a type of thine own varied lot,
The crown'd of genius, and the child of wo.
For at thy breast the ever-pointed thorn
Did gird itself in secret, mid the gush
Of such unstain'd, sublime, impassion'd song,
That angels, poising on some silver cloud,
Might listen mid the errands of the skies,
And linger all unblamed.

How tenderly
Doth Nature draw her curtain round thy rest,
And like a nurse, with finger on her lip,
Watch that no step disturb thee, and no hand
Profane thy sacred harp. Methinks she waits
Thy waking, as some cheated mother hangs
O'er the pale babe, whose spirit death hath stolen,
And laid it, dreaming, on the lap of Heaven.

Said we that thou art dead? We dare not. No.
For every mountain, stream, or shady dell
Where thy rich echoes linger, claim thee still,
Their own undying one. To thee was known
Alike the language of the fragile flower
And of the burning stars. God taught it thee.
So, from thy living intercourse with man,
Thou shalt not pass, until the weary earth
Drops her last gem into the doomsday flame.
Thou hast but taken thy seat with that bless'd choir,
Whose harmonies thy spirit learn'd so well
Through this low, darken'd casement, and so long
Interpreted for us.

Why should we say
Farewell to thee, since every unborn age
Shall mix thee with its household charities?
The hoary sire shall bow his deafen'd ear,
And greet thy sweet words with his benison;
The mother shrine thee as a vestal flame
In the lone temple of her sanctity;
And the young child who takes thee by the hand,
Shall travel with a surer step to Heaven.

THE WIDOW'S PRAYER.

The youthful maid, the gentle bride,
The happy wife, her husband's pride,
Who meekly kneel, at morning ray,
The incense of their vows to pay,
Or pour, amid their evening train,
From love's full heart, the incense-strain,
What know they of *her* anguish'd cry
Who lonely lifts the tearful eye?
No sympathizing glance to view
Her alter'd cheek's unearthly hue,
No soothing tone to quell the power
Of grief that bursts at midnight hour.
O God! her heart is pierced and bare,
Have pity on the widow's prayer.

Not like the mother, by whose side
The partner sits, her guard and guide,
Is she who, reft of earthly trust,
Hath laid her bosom's lord in dust.
Sleeps her young babe! but who shall share
Its waking charms, its holy care?
Who shield the daughter's opening bloom,
Whose father moulders in the tomb?
Her son the treacherous world beguiles,
What voice shall warn him of its wiles?
What strong hand break the deadly snare?
O answer, Heaven, the widow's prayer!

For not the breath of prosperous days,
Though warm with joy and wing'd with praise,
E'er kindled such a living coal
Of deep devotion in the soul
As that wild blast, which bore away
Her idol to returnless clay:
And, for the wreath that crown'd the brow,
Left bitter thoughts and hyssop-bough,
A lonely couch, a sever'd tie,
A tear that time can never dry,
Unutter'd wo, unpitied care:
O God! regard the widow's prayer.

"KEEP SILENCE."

A SABBATH HYMN.

Keep silence, pride! What dost thou here,
  With the frail sons of clay?
How darest thou in God's courts appear,
  Where contrite spirits pray?

Keep silence, wild and vexing care!
  Six measured days are thine,
Thy seed to sow, thy chaff to share,
  Steal not the day divine.

Keep silence, sorrow! Faith can tell
  With what sublime intent
Thou to the bosom's inmost cell
  By Heaven's right hand wert sent.

Keep silence, avarice! With thy hoard
  So boasted, yet so base,
Think'st thou the money-changer's board
  Hath here a fitting place?

Keep silence, vain and worldly joy,
  Foam on, time's tossing wave!
Why lure him with a treacherous toy
  Who trembles o'er the grave?

Keep silence, earth! the Lord is here,
  Thy great Creator blest!
His work of wisdom form'd thy sphere,
  Keep thou His day of rest.

ABRAHAM AT MACPELAH.

DEEP wrapp'd in shades
Olive and terebinth, its vaulted door
Fleck'd with the untrain'd vine and matted grass,
Behold Macpelah's cave.
Hark! hear we not
A voice of weeping? Lo, yon aged man
Bendeth beside his dead. Wave after wave
Of memory rises, till his lonely heart
Sees all its treasures floating on the flood,
Like rootless weeds.
The earliest dawn of love
Is present with him, and a form of grace,
Whose beauty held him ever in its thrall:
And then, the morn of marriage, gorgeous robes,
And dulcet music, and the rites that bless
The Eastern bride. Full many a glowing scene,
Made happy by her tenderness, returns
To mock his solitude, as the sharp lance
Severs the quivering nerve. His quiet home
Gleams through the oaks of Mamre. There he sat,
Rendering due rites of hospitality
To guests who bore the folded wing of Heaven
Beneath their vestments. And her smile was there,
Among the angels.
When her clustering curls
Wore Time's chill hoar-frost, with what glad surprise,

What holy triumph of exulting faith,
He saw fresh blooming in her wither'd arms
A fair young babe, the heir of all his wealth.
Forever blending with that speechless joy
Which thrill'd his soul, when first a father's name
Fell on his ear, is that pale, placid brow
O'er which he weeps.
                                        Yet had he seen it wear
Another semblance, tinged with hues of thought,
Perchance unlovely, in that trial-hour,
When to sad Hagur's mute, reproachful eye
He answer'd naught, but on her shoulder laid
The water-bottle and the loaf, and sent
Her and her son, unfriended wanderers, forth
Into the wilderness.
                                        Say, who can mourn
Over the smitten idol, by long years
Cemented with his being, yet perceive
No dark remembrance that he fain would blot,
Troubling the tear. If there were no kind deed
Omitted, no sweet healing word of love
Expected, yet unspoken ; no light tone
That struck discordant on the shivering nerve,
For which the weeper fain would rend the tomb
To cry forgive ! oh, let him kneel and praise
God amid all his grief.
                                        We may not say
If aught of penitence was in the pang
That wrung the labouring breast, while o'er the dust
Of Sarah, at Macpelah's waiting tomb,
The proud and princely Abraham bow'd him down,
A mourning stranger, mid the sons of Heth.

"JESUS OF NAZARETH PASSETH BY."

St. Luke, xviii., 39.

WATCHER, who wak'st by the bed of pain,
While the stars sweep on with their midnight train,
Stifling the tear for thy loved one's sake,
Holding thy breath lest her sleep should break,
In thy loneliest hour there's a helper nigh:
"Jesus of Nazareth passeth by."

Stranger, afar from thy native land,
Whom no one takes with a brother's hand,
Table and hearthstone are glowing free,
Casements are sparkling, but not for thee;
There is one who can tell of a home on high:
"Jesus of Nazareth passeth by."

Sad one, in secret bending low,
A dart in thy breast that the world may not know,
Wrestling the favour of God to win,
His seal of pardon for days of sin:
Press on, press on, with thy prayerful cry,
"Jesus of Nazareth passeth by."

Mourner, who sitt'st in the churchyard lone,
Scanning the lines on that marble stone,
Plucking the weeds from thy children's bed,
Planting the myrtle and rose instead,

Look up from the tomb with thy tearful eye,
"Jesus of Nazareth passeth by."

Fading one, with the hectic streak
In thy veins of fire and thy wasted cheek,
Fear'st thou the shade of the darken'd vale?
Look to the guide who can never fail:
He hath trod it himself! He will hear thy sigh,
"Jesus of Nazareth passeth by."

GOOD-NIGHT OF THE BIRDS.

It was a Sabbath evening
  In spring's most glorious time,
When tree, and shrub, and early flower
  Were in their fragrant prime;
And where the cloudless sun declined,
  A glow of light serene,
A blessing on the world he left,
  Came floating o'er the scene.

Then from the verdant hedgerow
  A gentle descant stole,
And with its tide of melody
  Dissolved the listening soul,
The tenants of that leafy lodge,
  Each in its downy nest,
Pour'd forth a fond and sweet "good-night"
  Before they sank to rest.

That tender parting carol!
  How wild it was, and deep,
And then, with soft, harmonious close,
  It melted into sleep;
Methought, in yonder land of praise,
  Which faith delights to view,
True-hearted, peaceful worshippers,
  There might be room for you.

Ye give us many a lesson
  Of music high and rare,
Sweet teachers of the lays of heaven,
  Say, will ye not be there?
Ye have no sins, like ours, to purge
  With penitential dew;
Oh! in the clime of perfect love,
  Is there no place for you?

THE DYING YEAR.

Voice of the Dying Year! I hear thy moan,
Like some spent breaker of the distant sea,
Chafing the fretted rock. Is this the end
Of thy fresh morning music, gushing out
In promises of hope? Have the bright flush
Of Spring's young beauty, crown'd with budding flowers,
The passion-vow of Summer, and the pledge
Of faithful, fruitful Autumn, come to this?
I see thy youngling moon go down the west,
The midnight clock gives warning, and its stroke
Must be thy death-knell. Is that quivering gasp
The last sad utterance of thine agony?
I see thy clay-cold fingers try to clasp
Some prop—in vain!

And so thou art no more.
No more! Thy rest is with oblivious years
Beyond the flood. Yet when the trump shall sound,
Blown by the strong archangel, thou shalt wake
From the dim sleep of ages. When the tombs
That lock their slumbering tenants cleave in twain,
Thou shalt come forth. Yea, thou shalt rise again,
And I shall look upon thee, when the dead
Stand before God. But come not murmuring forth,
Unwillingly, like Samuel's summon'd ghost,

To daunt me at the judgment. No; be kind,
Be pitiful, bear witness tenderly;
And if thou hast a dread account for me,
Go, dip thy dark scroll in redeeming blood.

HYMN AT SEA.

God of the ever-rolling deep,
  Our Father and our trust,
Who bidd'st its mighty billows sweep
  Around the born of dust,

Who bidd'st it towering o'er them raise
  Its everlasting walls,
Yet giv'st them slumber calm and sweet,
  As in their native halls,

God of the strong, unfathom'd tide,
  Whose pavement dark and drear,
The wrecks of human power and pride,
  Awake our trembling fear,

O grant us, as the lonely dove
  Unto the ark did flee,
Mid the hoarse tumult of the waves
  To rest secure in Thee.

THE DEPARTED FRIEND.

O Friend! the light is dead
In thy fair mansion, where in bright array
Love moved with buoyant tread,
And childhood's merry laughter, day by day,
Made the heart glad, and music lent its zest,
And hospitable smiles allured the welcome guest.

And in the holy place
A brow of beautiful and earnest thought,
A form of manly grace,
Are missing; and we gaze with sorrow fraught
Upon that vacant seat where beam'd for years
That spirit-speaking eye, the pastor's toil that cheers.

And from the couch of pain,
The cell of want, a voice hath pass'd away
Which sooth'd the suffering train,
And warn'd the smitten sinful man to pray;
Which, till the verge of life, with accents clear,
Told how a Christian's faith the hour of death can cheer.

O Friend! how great thy gain,
Thus borne in manhood's vigour to the skies,
Ere age or wasting pain
Had chill'd the full fount of thy sympathies,
Those sympathies that still with ardent glow
Joy'd at another's joy, or mourn'd for other's wo.

Hast thou embraced *them* there,
Thy kindred, tenants of yon world of bliss?
Oh say, do angels share
The sympathies so sweetly sown in this?
The nurtured 'neath one roof, one native sky,
Meet they with changeless love where every tear is dry?

Ah! hast thou seen *his* face
Whom thy young hand with tender zeal did lead
To seek a Saviour's grace?
That brother, who, God's flock ordain'd to feed,
Touch'd with pure lip the altar's living fire,
And earlier found his place with Heaven's immortal choir.

Say, at the pearly gate
Hail'd *she* thy coming with a fond acclaim;
She who, with hope elate,
Taught thy young lisping tongue the Almighty's name?
And he, whose life closed like a hymn of praise,
Thy patriarchal sire, serene and full of days?

Be silent; ask no more;
Bow in deep reverence to the sacred dead;
No mortal thought may soar
To their high ecstasy, unnamed and dread;
Wait till the temple's veil is rent for thee,
And let God's will be thine, heir of eternity.

L

HEAVEN'S LESSON.

HEAVEN teacheth thee to mourn, O friend beloved;
Thou art its pupil now. The lowest class,
The first beginners in its school, may learn
How to rejoice. The sycamore's broad leaf,
Thrill'd by the breeze, the humblest grass-bird's nest,
Murmur of gladness, and the wondering babe,
Borne by its nurse out in the open fields,
Knoweth that lesson. The wild mountain-stream
That throws by fits its gushing music forth,
The careless sparrow, happy, though the frosts
Nip his light foot, have learn'd the simple lore
How to rejoice. Mild Nature teacheth it
To all her innocent works.
But God alone
Instructeth how to mourn. He doth not trust
This highest lesson to a voice or hand
Subordinate. Behold! He cometh forth!
O sweet disciple, bow thyself to learn
The alphabet of tears. Receive the lore,
Sharp though it be, to an unanswering breast,
A will subdued. And may such wisdom spring
From these rough rudiments, that thou shalt gain
A class more noble, and, advancing, soar
Where the sole lesson is a seraph's praise.
Yea, be a docile scholar, and so rise
Where mourning hath no place.

DEATH OF A FATHER.

Say, shall we render thanks for him
  Whose sorrows all are o'er?
Whose footsteps leave the storm-wash'd sands
  Of this terrestrial shore?
Who to the garner of the bless'd,
  In yon immortal land,
Was gather'd, as the ripen'd sheaf
  Doth meet the reaper's hand?

Yet precious was that reverend man,
  And to his arm I clung,
Till more than fourscore weary years
  Their shadows o'er him flung;
Not lonely or unloved he dwelt,
  Though earliest friends had fled,
For sweet affections sprang anew
  When older roots were dead.

There lies the Holy Book of God,
  His oracle and guide,
Where last my children read to him,
  The page still open wide;
Yet where he bent to hear their voice
  Is but a vacant chair,
A lone staff standing by its side:
  They call—he is not there!

He is not there, my little ones!
  So suddenly he fled,
They cannot bring it to their minds
  That he is of the dead.
Yet oft the hymns he sang with them,
  So tunefully and slow,
Shall wake sad echo in their souls,
  Like parting tones of wo.

There was his favourite noonday seat,
  Beneath yon trellised vine,
To mark the embryo clusters swell,
  The aspiring tendrils twine;
Or, lightly leaning on his staff,
  With vigorous step he went
A little way among the flowers,
  With morning dews besprent.

How dear was every rising sun
  That cloudless met his eye,
And, nightly, how his graceful prayer
  Rose upward, warm and high;
For freely to his God he gave
  The blossom of his prime,
So He forgot him not amid
  The water-floods of time.

The cherish'd memories of the past,
  How strong they burn'd, and clear,
Prompting the tale the listening boy
  Still held his breath to hear,

How a young cradled nation woke
  To grasp the glittering brand,
And strangely raise the half-knit arm
  To brave the mother-land.

Those stormy days! those stormy days!
  When, with a fearful cry,
The blood-stain'd earth at Lexington
  Invoked the avenging sky,
When in the scarce-drawn furrow
  The farmer's plough was stay'd,
And for the gardener's pruning-hook
  Sprang forth the warrior's blade.

The glorious deeds of Washington,
  The chiefs of other days!
Another lip is silent now
  That used to speak their praise;
Another link is stricken
  From the living chain that bound
The legends of an ancient race
  Our thrilling hearts around.

We gaze on where the patriarchs stood
  In ripen'd virtue strong,
How shall we dare to fill the place
  That they have fill'd so long?
How on the bosoms of our race
  Enforce the truths they breathed,
Or wear that mantle of the skies
  They to our souls bequeathed?

But ah! to think that breast is cold,
  Whose sympathetic tone
Responded to my joys and woes
  As though they were its own,
To know the prayer that was my guard,
  My pilot o'er the sea,
Must never, in this vale of tears,
  Be lifted more for me.

There was no frost upon his hair,
  No anguish on his brow,
Those bright brown locks, my pride and care,
  Methinks I see them now;
Methinks that beaming smile I see,
  In love and patience sweet,
O father! must that smile no more
  My quicken'd footsteps greet?

Yet wrong we not that messenger
  Who gather'd back the breath,
Calling him ruthless spoiler, stern,
  And fell destroyer, death?
His touch was like the angel's
  Who comes at close of day
To lull the willing flowers asleep
  Until the morning ray.

And so they laid the righteous man
  'Neath the green turf to rest,
And blessed were the words of prayer
  That fell upon his breast;

For sure it were an ingrate's deed
  To murmur or repine,
That such a life, my sire, was closed
  By such as death as thine.

But thou, our God, who know'st our frame,
  Whose shield is o'er us spread,
When every idol of our love
  Is desolate and dead,
Father and mother may forsake,
  Yet be Thou still our trust,
And let thy chastenings cleanse the soul
  From vanity and dust.

"OREMUS."*

OREMUS. Lo, the infant morn
Is in the curtain'd orient born,
And fleet the volumed mists away
Before th' exulting eye of day.
High soar the birds, the groves rejoice,
Mute Nature smiles to hear their voice,
Smiles through the crystal streams that shine,
And through the flowers their banks that line.
O man, creation's noblest heir,
Pour'st thou to God no grateful prayer?
Lift up the heart, his word believe,
And freely as ye ask, receive.

Oremus. Noon is riding high,
The manhood of the day is nigh,
The hour of fervour and of care;
Haste where cool shades thy strength repair,
Where clustering vines, and boughs that weep,
Shall lull thy weariness to sleep.
Know'st thou that cordial balm to gain
Which sooths the broken spirit's pain?
Know'st thou where grows the living bread?
Where Heaven's unrusting gold is spread?
Where hides the spell that heals the blind?
Go, seek the key of Heaven, and find.

* "Let us pray."

Oremus. Twilight's pensive eye
Peers o'er the bulwark of the sky,
The night-watch of the stars is set,
The gibbous moon the clouds hath met,
That o'er her disk, with anger pale,
In playful arrogance prevail.
Day seals her casket close, to wait
For the last judgment's awful fate ;
If pardon for thine erring deed,
Or guardian o'er thy couch there need,
Knock, and the gate of Heaven shall be
Thrown open to thy wants and thee.

Oremus : till the glittering store
Of youth and hope delude no more,
Till ripen'd years have stolen away,
And hermit age with temples gray,
And tottering staff, and vacant air,
Shall lead thee on, thou know'st not where,
Till he who wields the mortal sting
His never-erring shaft shall wing,
Crush the weak clay in ruins dread,
The cistern break with dew-drops fed,
Oremus : till seraphic lays
Turn prayer's imploring tone to praise.

RETURN OF THE PARENTS.

Long had they sped
O'er distant hill and valley, noting much
God's goodness in the riches of the land,
The summer fruitage, and the harvest hoard,
The reaper, wrestling with the bearded wheat,
And the proud torrent's glory, when it shakes
The everlasting rock, nor yet forgets
To sprinkle greenness on the lowliest flower,
All trembling at its base. Much, too, they spake
Of pleasure 'neath the hospitable roof
Of sever'd kindred ; how the quicken'd heart
Wins, from such meetings, power to wipe away
The dust of household care, which sometimes hangs
In clouds o'er the clear spirit.
But anon
The eloquent lip grew silent, for they drew
Near that bless'd spot which throws all other lights
Into strong shadow—*home!*
At that dear thought
The bosom's pulse beat wildly, and the wheels
Were all too slow, though scarce the eager steeds
Obey'd the rein. And, as the mother spake
Somewhat in murmurs of her youngest boy,
There came a flood of beauty o'er her brow—
For holy love hath beauty—which gray time
Could never steal.

'Tis there, behind the trees,
That well-known roof: and from the open door
What a glad rush! The son, who fain would take
His mother in his arms, as if her foot
Was all too good for earth; and at his side
The beautiful daughter, with her raven hair
So smoothly folded o'er her classic brow;
The infant, crowing in its nurse's arms;
The bold boy, in his gladness springing up
Even to his father's shoulder; lisping tongues,
And little dancing feet, and outstretch'd hands
Grasping the parents' skirts: it was a group
That artist's pencil never yet hath sketch'd
In all its plenitude.

And when I saw
The brightness of the tear of joy, I felt
How poor the pomp of princes, and the dross
Of beaten gold, compared with that dear wealth—
Home, and its gratulations, and the ties
Which Heaven hath twisted round congenial souls,
To draw them to itself.

PELICAN ON THE SEA OF GALILEE.

"A single pelican was floating there; like myself, he was alone."—*Stephens's Incidents of Travel.*

LONE bird, upon yon sacred sea,
  Dimpling with solitary breast
The silent wave of Galilee,
  Where shall thine oary foot find rest?

Hast thou a home mid rock or reed
  Of this most desolate domain,
Where not one ibex dares to feed,
  Nor Arab tent imprints the plain?

What know'st thou of Bethsaida's gate?
  Or old Chorazin's desert bound?
What heed'st thou of Capernaum's fate,
  Whose shapeless ruins throng around?

Once, when the tempest's wing was dark,
  A sleeper rose and calm'd the sea,
And snatch'd from death the fragile bark—
  Here was the spot, but who was he?

He heard the surge impetuous roar,
  And trod sublime its wildest crest,
Redeemer! was yon watery floor
  Thus by thy glorious feet impress'd?

Oh, when each earthly hope and fear,
  Each fleeting loss, each fancied gain,
Shall to our death-dimm'd sight appear
  Like the lost cities of the plain,

Then may the soul, enslaved no more,
  Launch calmly on salvation's sea,
And part from time's receding shore,
  Lone, peaceful pelican! like thee.

M

THE PAST.

" God requireth that which is past."—*Ecclesiastes.*

THE Past! We have forgotten it:
Its shadowy reign is o'er,
And like a folded mist hangs
O'er dim oblivion's shore;
The deeds of childhood's distant day,
Light words from youth that fell,
Unnumber'd thoughts of ripen'd years,
Who can their import tell?

The Present, with its strong embrace,
Our prison'd heart detains,
The Future lures us blindfold on
By Hope's illusive chains:
But who to woo the hoary Past,
That old and wither'd crone,
Turns with a lover's ardent eye,
Or an enthusiast's tone?

Yet Heaven records, though we forget,
Each deed that shuns the light,
Each word that melted into air,
And hid from memory's sight;
The very thoughts that in their birth
Sank motionless and dead,
All have their impress on that page
Which at God's bar is read.

The Present, like an eagle's wing,
  May from our vision fleet,
The Future, in its robe of dreams,
  Our grasp may never meet;
But, frail one, with the fearful Past
  Mysterious secrets are,
Oh, spread thy conscience to thy Judge
  In penitence and prayer.

THE HEATH IN THE DESERT.

" He shall be like the heath in the desert, and shall not see when good cometh."—*Jeremiah*, xvii., 6.

There falls a bless'd rain on the desolate scene,
The long-withered herbage is healthful and green,
New verdure replaces the bramble and thorn,
In dry, sterile regions fresh fountains are born.
The murmur of streamlets rejoices the ear—
Wake, heath of the desert! salvation is near.

There breathes a soft wind o'er the bones of the slain,
It hath clothed them with flesh, they are living again;
Like the host of the Lord, in bright armour they stand,
Their banners wave wide at His word of command,
The wilderness smiles on their glorious array—
Wake, heath of the desert! and gladden their way.

There sweeps a dark cloud o'er the blue of the sky,
Hoarse thunders are muttering, the tempest draws nigh,
The chariot of God rolleth on in its ire,
The mountains are humbled, the valleys aspire,
Lo, the scorner and slumberer their folly deplore—
Wake, heath of the desert! ere time be no more.

HYMN IN SICKNESS.

THIS life, with all its thousand ties,
  Is but a loan from Thee
Our God, whose wisdom framed the skies,
  Whose strength controls the sea.

Thine are its early joys, that spring
  Like flowers where'er we tread,
And thine its later comforts too,
  When morning hopes are fled.

Thou Maker of this feeble frame,
  Who know'st its every pain,
And bidd'st its broken wheels roll on
  When man's poor help is vain,

Still plainly as thy power is seen,
  Thy bless'd compassions shine,
So would we peaceful rest our souls
  Upon thine arm divine,

And, clinging to our Saviour's cross,
  Supported by His love,
Pass through this changeful life below,
  To deathless life above.

REQUEST OF THE DYING CHILD.

STRETCH'D on the couch of pain, there lay a child
Of some few summers. The dense city's roofs
Throng'd thick around her, and the vertic sun
Pour'd from those glowing tiles a fervid heat
Upon her shrinking nerves. Sad she retraced
The rural scenes where her young childhood grew,
And wishfully her pale lips shaped the sound
Of *home, sweet home.*

"Dear mother, take me there,
To that first home. The early flowers that sprung
Beside the garden walk, and those tall trees,
Would I might see them but once more, and touch
The pleasant vine that o'er my window climb'd.
I could breathe freer there."

And so they raised
The languid child, for how could they deny
Her last heart-yearning? and with mournful tears
Wrapp'd as a traveller her whom Death had seal'd
For his returnless journey.

Swift the boat
Shot o'er the river-tide, and then the wheel,
Careful yet tedious, mark'd the well-known track
O'er hill and valley. Patiently she bore
The weary travel, and when sunset brought
The well-remember'd haunt, upraised her head,
And with a tremulous and tender tone

Hail'd each familiar object. It would seem
As if, indulgent to her fond request,
Death waited for her. Though the thread-like pulse
Stirr'd not the ivory arm, and the poor heart
Scarce forced the life-tide oozing drop by drop,
Yet still Death waited for her.

One full hour
She lay within his icy arms, and drew
In deep, long, quivering gasps her native air.
He waited for her while she grasp'd the flowers,
The fresh wild-flowers that bloom'd where she was born,
And while she gazed upon the waving trees,
And press'd the fragrant vine-leaves to her brow.
But then he coldly beckon'd her away:
And so she meekly kiss'd her mother's lips,
And went to rest.

How sweet that home to thee
From whence is no departure, peaceful child!
And where no pilgrim with his dusty staff
Toils just to gaze upon its blissful gate,
Then turn and die.

And they who fed thee here
With love's rich balm-cup, let it be their joy,
Their hymn of gratulation night and day,
That thou art gather'd with the pure in heart,
Back to thy natural element again.

THE CHURCH BELL.

When glowing in the eastern sky,
The Sabbath morning meets the eye,
And o'er a weary, care-worn scene,
Gleams like the ark-dove's leaf of green,
How welcome over hill and dale,
Thy hallow'd summons loads the gale,
Sweet bell! Church bell!

When earthly joys and sorrows end,
And towards our long repose we tend,
How mournfully thy tone doth call
The weepers to the funeral,
And to the last abode of clay,
With solemn knell mark out the way,
Sad bell! Church bell!

If to the clime where pleasures reign,
We through a Saviour's love attain,
If freshly to an angel's thought,
Earth's unforgotten scenes are brought,
Will not thy voice, that warn'd to prayer,
Be gratefully remember'd there,
Bless'd bell? Church bell?

THE BUTTERFLY.

A BUTTERFLY bask'd on a baby's grave,
Where a lily had chanced to grow:
"Why art thou here, with thy gaudy die,
When she of the blue and sparkling eye,
Must sleep in the churchyard low?"

Then it lightly soar'd through the sunny air,
And spoke from its shining track:
"I was a worm till I won my wings,
And she whom thou mourn'st like a seraph sings:
Wouldst thou call the bless'd one back?"

MONODY TO MRS. SARAH L. SMITH.

So Asia hath thy dust, thou who wert born
Amid my own wild hillocks, where the voice
Of falling waters and of gentle gales
Mingle their music. How thy soft dark eye,
Thy graceful form, thy soul-illumined smile,
Gleam forth upon me when I muse at eve,
Mid the bright imagery of earliest years.

Hear I the murmur'd echo of thy name
From yon poor forest race? 'Tis meet for them
To hoard thy memory as a blessed star,
For thou didst seek their lowly homes, and tell
Their sad-brow'd children of a Saviour's love,
And of a clime where no oppressor comes.
Cold winter found thee there, and summer's heat,
With zeal unblenching. Though perchance the sneer
Might curl some worldling's lip, 'twas not for thee
To note its language, or to scorn the soul
Of the neglected Indian, or to tread
Upon the ashes of his buried kings
As on a loathsome weed.

Thine own fair halls
Lured thee in vain, until the hallow'd church
Rear'd its light dome among them, and the voice
Of a devoted shepherd, day by day,
Call'd back those wanderers to the sheltering fold
Of a Redeemer's righteousness.

THE BUTTERFLY.

A butterfly bask'd on a baby's grave,
  Where a lily had chanced to grow:
"Why art thou here, with thy gaudy die,
When she of the blue and sparkling eye,
  Must sleep in the churchyard low?"

Then it lightly soar'd through the sunny air,
  And spoke from its shining track:
"I was a worm till I won my wings,
And she whom thou mourn'st like a seraph sings:
  Wouldst thou call the bless'd one back?"

MONODY TO MRS. SARAH L. SMITH.

So Asia hath thy dust, thou who wert born
Amid my own wild hillocks, where the voice
Of falling waters and of gentle gales
Mingle their music. How thy soft dark eye,
Thy graceful form, thy soul-illumined smile,
Gleam forth upon me when I muse at eve,
Mid the bright imagery of earliest years.

Hear I the murmur'd echo of thy name
From yon poor forest race? 'Tis meet for them
To hoard thy memory as a blessed star,
For thou didst seek their lowly homes, and tell
Their sad-brow'd children of a Saviour's love,
And of a clime where no oppressor comes.
Cold winter found thee there, and summer's heat,
With zeal unblenching. Though perchance the sneer
Might curl some worldling's lip, 'twas not for thee
To note its language, or to scorn the soul
Of the neglected Indian, or to tread
Upon the ashes of his buried kings
As on a loathsome weed.
                                        Thine own fair halls
Lured thee in vain, until the hallow'd church
Rear'd its light dome among them, and the voice
Of a devoted shepherd, day by day,
Call'd back those wanderers to the sheltering fold
Of a Redeemer's righteousness.

And then
Thy path was on the waters, and thy hand
Close clasp'd in his who bore so fearless forth
The glorious Gospel to those ancient climes
Which in the darkness and the shade of death
Benighted dwell.
Strong ties detain'd thee here:
Home—father—sightless mother—sister dear—
Brothers and tender friends—a full array
Of hope and bliss. But what were those to thee,
Who on God's altar laid the thought of self?
What were such joys to thee, if duty bade
Their crucifixion ?
Oh! Jerusalem!
Jerusalem! Say, do I see thee there?
Pondering the flinty path thy Saviour trod,
Or fervent kneeling where his prayer arose,
All night on Olivet? or with meek hand
Culling from pure Siloam's marge a flower,
Whose tender leaflets drink as fresh a dew
As when unhumbled Judah wore the crown
Of queenly beauty? or with earnest eye
Exploring where the shepherd-minstrel kept
His father's flock, before the cares that lodge
Within the thorn-wreath'd circlet of a king
Had turn'd his temples gray? or with sweet smile
Reposing, wearied, in thy simple tent
By turbid Jordan and the bitter wave
Of the Asphaltites?
Back to thy place
Amid the Syrian vales, to thy loved toils
For the forsaken Druses, to the throng

Of heathen babes, who on thine accents hang
As on a mother's ; for the time is short.
Perils upon the waters wait for thee,
And then another Jordan, from whose flood
Is no return.
But thou, with lip so pale,
Didst take the song of triumph, and go down
Alone and fearless through its depths profound.
Snatches of heavenly harpings made thee glad,
Even to thy latest gasp.
Therefore the grief
Born at thy grave is not like other grief.
Tears mix with joy. We praise our God for thee.

A FATHER'S PITY.

"Like as a father pitieth his children."—*David.*

How doth a father pity?
See the snare
Of loathsome vice around his son entwine;
Behold his mournful mien, his anxious air;
List to his earnest cry for aid divine;
Precept on precept pour'd, and line on line,
To snatch the victim from a gulf profound;
And should those steps once more to peace incline,
How do the parent's lips with praise resound,
As swell the heavenly harps when a lost soul is found.

How doth a father pity?
Ask the form
That feebly on his sheltering bosom lies,
Like smitten lily shrinking from the storm,
Consumption's signal in her languid eyes;
What torturing sympathies within him rise,
When the fierce cough awakes with racking throe,
And to her cheek the burning hectic flies,
How is his manly breast surcharged with wo
To see his darling hope, like fading flower, laid low.

How doth a father pity?
Mark his face
Bow'd in deep anguish o'er his cradled heir,
Faint struggling in the ice of death's embrace,
With ceaseless moaning and convulsive stare,

Reproachful calling on the parents' care
To ease its pangs; fain would those hearts that burst
Their lamblike nursling's mortal misery bear:
So doth *He* pity us who is our trust,
The Former of our frame, remembering we are dust.

MIDNIGHT THOUGHTS AT SEA.

Borne upon the ocean's foam,
Far from native land and home,
Midnight's curtain dense with wrath,
Brooding o'er our venturous path,
While the mountain wave is rolling,
And the ship's bell faintly tolling:
Saviour! on the boisterous sea,
Bid us rest secure in Thee.

Blast and surge conflicting hoarse,
Sweep us on with headlong force,
And the bark which tempests urge,
Moans and trembles at their scourge;
Yet, if wildest tempests swell,
Be thou near, and all is well.
Saviour! on the stormy sea,
Let us find repose in Thee.

Hearts there are with love that burn,
When to us afar they turn;
Eyes that show the rushing tear
If our utter'd names they hear:
Saviour! o'er the faithless main,
Bring us to those homes again,
As the trembler, touch'd by Thee,
Safely trod the treacherous sea.

N 2

Wrecks are darkly spread below,
Where with lonely keel we go ;
Gentle brows and bosoms brave
Those abysses richly pave ;
If beneath the briny deep
We, with them, should coldly sleep,
Saviour ! o'er the whelming sea,
Take our ransom'd souls to Thee.

CHANGES.

Come to thy native village, thou, who long
Hast been a denizen of richer climes
And prouder cities. Nature all adorn'd
Welcomes thee back, and, like a peasant-friend
Exulting, filleth at her cottage-door
The beechen cup, with honey'd balm, for thee.
She fain would tell thee tales of every change
In her slight drama since thou last wert here,
Though none her scene hath shifted, or exchanged
Her honest-hearted actors, save gray Time,
Scattering the elm-leaves o'er the russet walk,
Or to the seedling in its bed of mould,
Whispering that spring hath come. She bids thee seek
Thy favourite brook, while Memory, ancient crone,
Waiteth to point thee where thy tiny boat
Or water-wheel sped gayly, or to show
The broader pool, upon whose icy glade
Thy foot was fleetest, while thy merry voice
Rang like a bugle when the shout was high.
See'st thou yon blooming creature, sweetly deck'd
With all the grace of perfect womanhood?
Lo, thou hast taken her ofttimes in thine arms,
When but a few brief moons had o'er her roll'd,
And sang to please her, though the watchful nurse
Was fain to snatch her from thine untaught hand,
Fearing thy whisker'd cheek might frighten her.

Thou canst not think so many years have fled
Since those good times ; and yet as silently
As the light snowflake glide our fleeting days,
And, while we dream their greenness still survives,
Amid the remnant of their wither'd pride
Our steps make sullen echo.
But 'tis weak
To mourn the change that nature writes on man,
As heavenly wisdom dictates. Doth the sheaf
Look back regretful to its bursting germe ?
Or the ripe fruit bemoan the fallen flower ?
Why then should man lament his vanish'd morn ?
The day of duty is the day of joy ;
Of highest joy, such as the heavens do bless.
So keep perpetual summer in thy soul,
And take the spirit's smile along with thee,
Even to thy winding-sheet.
Yon lowly roof,
Thou know'st it well, and yet it seems more low
Than it was wont to seem ; for thou hast been
A visitant of loftier domes, and halls
Meet for the feet of princes. Ask thou not
For father or for mother, they who made
That humble home so beautiful to thee :
But go thy way, and show to some young heart
The same deep love, the same unchanging zeal
Of pure example, pointing to the skies
That nurtured thee. So shalt thou pay the debt
To nature's best affections and to God.

THE FIRESIDE.

"Say, what have you brought to our own fireside?"
  'Twas a mother's voice that spake:
"The wintry tempest doth loudly chide,
But peace and joy shall with us abide—
  Oh, cherish them for my sake.

"A common stock is our happiness here:
  Each heart must contribute its mite
The bliss to swell or the pain to cheer;
Husband, and son, and daughter dear,
  What have you brought to-night?"

Then the studious boy, from his storied page,
  Look'd up with a thoughtful eye:
That knowledge gleam'd thence which doth charm the
    sage,
And shine like a flame through the frost of age
  With warmth and majesty.

A girl was there, like a rose on its stem,
  And her sacred song she pour'd:
Beauty and music, a blended gem,
Shook from their sparkling diadem,
  To enrich the evening hoard.

By a pale, sick child was a treasure brought,
The smile of patient trust,
For disease had a precious moral wrought,
And quiet and pure was her chasten'd thought,
As a pearl by the rude sea nursed.

An infant rose from its cradle-bed,
And clung to the mother's breast,
But soon to the knee of its sire it sped—
Love was its gift—and the angels said
That the baby's gift was best.

Then the father spake, with a grateful air,
Of the God whom his youth had known;
And the mother's sigh of tender care
Went up in the shape of a winged prayer,
And was heard before the Throne.

SEED FOR HEAVEN.

THE boy sat listening to the words
  That from his mother fell,
Pure lessons, wrapp'd in gentle tones,
  Like music's softest swell.

And oft he mark'd her musing brow,
  With holy silence bright,
And bless'd its placid smile, and deem'd
  That angels loved the sight.

Yet when that mother laid her down
  To rest in mouldering clay,
The world's temptations o'er him roll'd,
  And swept his faith away.

Like bird that scorns the fowler's snare,
  He trifled with his fate,
Forgot to seek the Spirit's aid,
  Or for its teachings wait.

Yet once, as in his midnight watch,
  The lonely deck he paced,
With naught but solemn stars above,
  And, round, old Ocean's waste,

Methought *her* warning voice, who long
'Neath the cold sods had slept,
Spake forth from every rushing wave
That on resistless swept;

Methought a teardrop, like her own,
Fell from the gathering cloud,
That round the slowly-rising moon
Had wreath'd its silver shroud;

Methought the searching eye of God
Flamed in his secret soul,
And down the proud man bow'd, with tears,
To own its strong control:

The Saviour's lowly yoke he took,
His flinty heart was riven,
And so the seed his mother sow'd
Brought forth rich fruit for Heaven.

DREAMS.

Revere the mind, so full of mystery,
Even in its passive hours.
Behold it roam,
With unseal'd eye and wide unfolded wing,
While the tired body sleeps. Immortal guest!
Our earthly nature bows itself to thee,
Pressing its ear of flesh unto the sigh
Of thy perturbed visions, if perchance
It hear some murmur of thy birth divine,
Thy deathless heritage.
Ah! dreams are dear
To those whom waking life hath surfeited
With dull monotony. When the long day
Wends to its close, and stealthy evening steals,
Like some lean miser, greedily to snatch
Hope's wreath that morning gave, is it not sweet
To close our eyelids, and to find the rose
That hides no thorn, the gold that knows no rust,
Scatter'd where'er we tread? Is it not sweet
To 'scape from stern reality, and glide
Where'er wild fancy marks her fairy way
Unlimited? If adverse fortune make
Our pillow stony, like the patriarch's bed
At lonely Bethel, do not pitying dreams
Plant a bright ladder for the angels' feet,
And change our hard couch to the gate of Heaven,

And feed our souls on manna, till they loathe
Their household bread?
To traverse all unblamed
Broad realms, more bright than fabled Araby;
To hear unearthly music; to inhale
Ambrosial fragrance from the spicy groves
That never fade; to see the tyrant tomb
Unlock its treasure-valve, and freely yield
The loved, the lost, back to our glad embrace;
To catch clear glimpses of the streets of gold,
And harpers harping mid the eternal hills,
These are the pastimes which the mind doth take
While its poor clay companion slumbers deep,
Weary and worn.
If thou in wintry climes
Shouldst exiled roam, thy very heart's blood chill'd,
Lay but thy cold hand on a winged dream,
And it shall bear thee straight with bounding pulse
To drink the sunbeams of thine own blue skies,
Where the young cottage children freely fill
Their pinafores with flowers.
Should ocean swell,
Or the eternal mountains stretch their bars
'Tween thee and thy loved home, how strangely sweet
To touch the talisman of dreams, and sit
Again on thine own sofa, hand in hand
With the most loved, thy children near thy side
At their untiring play, the shaded lamp
Shedding its quiet beam, while now and then
The clock upon the mantelpiece doth speak,
To register the diamond sands of time,
Made brighter by thy joys.

So mayst thou hold
Existence in two hemispheres, and be
Happy in both ; yea, in each separate zone
Have thine own castles, and revisit them
Whene'er it pleaseth thee.

But more than this :
If thou wilt seek the fellowship of dreams,
And fearless yield thee to their loving sway,
And make them friends, they'll swiftly bear thee up
From star to star, and let thee hear the rush
Of angel-wings, upon God's errands speeding ;
And, while they make some silver cloud thy car,
Will whispering tell thee that the unslumbering soul
Wears immortality upon its crest,
And, by its very power to soar with them,
Proves that it cannot die.

WIFE OF A MISSIONARY AT HER HUSBAND'S GRAVE.

THERE was a new-made grave,
  On a far heathen shore,
Where lonely slept a man of God,
  His mission-service o'er;
There, when the setting sun
  Had tinged the west with flame,
A tender infant in her arms,
  A mournful woman came.

Her youthful cheek was pale,
  Her fair form bending low,
As thus upon the fitful gale
  She pour'd her plaint of wo:
"Friend of my inmost soul,
  The turf is on thy breast,
And here amid the stranger's land
  Thy precious dust must rest.

"Our helpless babe I bring,
  Who knew no father's love,
Nor look'd upon this world of pain
  Till thou hadst risen above;
I lay him on thy bed,
  Unconscious tears to weep,
Before our last farewell we take,
  And dare the faithless deep.

"Oh, when the mountain wave
Shall be our venturous path,
And the loud midnight tempest howls
In terror and in wrath,
Thy manly arm no more
My dearest prop must be,
Nor thy strong counsel nerve my soul
To brave the raging sea.

"But if our native coast
Once more these feet should tread,
And thou, the life of all my joys,
Be absent with the dead,
While each remember'd scene
Shall with thine image glow,
And friend and parent name thy name,
How shall I bear the wo?

"Is it thy voice, my love,
That bids me bear the rod,
And stay my desolated heart
Upon the widow's God?
Say'st thou, when every ray
Of hope is quench'd and dim,
The widow and the fatherless
May put their trust in Him?

"How bless'd that Word Divine,
On which my soul relies,
The resurrection of the just,
The union in the skies!"

Faith came with heavenly light,
  Her struggling grief to quell,
And in the holy words of prayer
  She spake her last farewell.

SABBATH MEDITATIONS.

Toss'd on the angry deep, with riven sails,
  The bark, long struggling 'gainst the tempest's wrath,
Meets the rich perfume breathed from land-born gales,
  And skims more lightly o'er her billowy path ;
While the glad sailor marks the misty line
Where his loved native hills the blue horizon join.

Spent, on his broken raft, the swimmer lies,
  A noteless speck mid ocean's stormy spray,
While round his head the shrieking seagull flies,
  And warns her comrades of the expected prey ;
See ! see ! the lifeboat ! Lo, its deck he gains,
And mid protecting friends forgets his fearful pains.

The traveller, faint amid the desert sands,
  Thinks of his native clime with bitter tear,
Fast by his side his drooping camel stands,
  Hark to the cry of hope ! a fountain near !
A green oasis mid the burning plain,
And 'neath the palm-tree shade he dreams of home again.

And art not thou, O glorious Sabbath morn,
  A lifeboat to the outcast on the main ?
A sight of home to mariner forlorn ?
  A sound of waters mid the burning plain ?

Bear to my soul thy blessing from on high,
That dayspring of our God whose beams shall never die.

With holy words of psalmist and of seer,
  With penitential prayers in secret born,
With chant and worship of the temple dear,
  Come thou to me, O consecrated morn;
Descend and touch devotion's slumbering chord,
And tell to listening faith the rising of her Lord.

Yes, raise me o'er the dust and care of life,
  A little way towards that celestial seat,
Where, freed for aye from vanity and strife,
  The "just made perfect" in communion meet;
Show me their vestments gleaming from the sky,
Pour through heaven's opening gate their echoed minstrelsy,

And I will thank thee, though to earth I turn,
  And all too soon from thy bless'd precepts stray,
Though in my breast its fever-thirst should burn,
  And storm or shipwreck daunt my venturous way,
Still will I grasp thee as a golden chain,
And bind thee to my heart until we meet again.

THE SACRED POET.

Art thou a mouth for the immortal mind?
A voice that shall be heard when ages sleep
In cold oblivion? when the rich man's pomp,
And all the ambitious strivings of the crowd
Shall be forgotten? Art thou well convinced
That such a gift is thine?
Bow thee to dust,
And take this honour from the hand of God
In deep humility, worm as thou art,
And all unworthy. Ask for naught beside,
Though worldlings scorn thy lot.
Prosperity,
Such as earth names, what are its gauds to thee?
Accustom'd to the crystal and the gold
Of poesy, that, like a sea of glass,
Doth compass thee around. Look up! look up!
Baptized and set apart for Heaven's high will,
Search for its lessons. List when trembling dawn
Instructs Aurora; muse when night to night
Doth show forth knowledge; when the folded flower
Taketh its lesson of the dews that steal
Into its bosom, like the mother's hymn
O'er the tired infant; and thine ear shall drink
A music-tone to solace every wound
That earth has made.
Then strike thy hallow'd harp
For unborn ages, and with trumpet-tone

Wake the immortal mind to highest hopes,
And be the teacher of what cannot die.
Yea, wear thy birthright nobly on thy brow,
And nerve the wing for God.

THE MAY-FLOWER.*

A SPECK amid the ocean,
  A laden bark draws near,
Through her rent sails the bleak winds moan,
  All heavily and drear;
No light upon the headlands
  Illumes her dangerous way,
No pilot-boat all fearless glides
  Like sea-bird o'er the spray.

Slow, towards a sterile region,
  With pain she seems to steer,
No hoarded treasures in her breast,
  To grasping avarice dear;
Yet many a noble galleon,
  Where Indian jewels sleep,
Might pave old ocean's glittering floor,
  Without a loss so deep.

No broad flag proudly waveth,
  No banner from her mast,
But many a princely argosy
  Might feel the wrecking blast;

* The name of the vessel from which the Pilgrim-fathers first landed at Plymouth, in December, 1620.

Or, crush'd by battle-thunders, sink
  'Neath whelming waters dark,
Yet leave no chasm on History's page,
  Like yon forsaken bark.

Oh, May-Flower! stricken May-Flower!
  So scourged by Winter's wrath,
What bear'st thou to this chilling clime,
  Along thy billowy path?
And the May-Flower boldly answer'd,
  As towards the shore she drew,
"*Seed for a nation of the free,*
  Unblenching souls and true."

Hoarse voices from the wilderness
  Spake out when storms were high,
"Were there no graves beyond the main,
  That here ye come to die?"
But sweetly on the Sabbath breeze
  An answering anthem peal'd,
"Our leader is the Lord of Hosts,
  Our fortress and our shield."

Down sank the ancient forest,
  And up the roof-tree sprang,
The tall corn ripen'd on the lea,
  The soldier's watchword rang;
Gaunt Famine, like a hungry wolf,
  Was stoutly held at bay,
And the mother lull'd her wailing babe
  With England's holy lay.

Rich was each lowly cabin
  In the strong trust of prayer,
A heaven-born might to brave the lot
  Of poverty and care;
So now a glorious nation
  Doth rise in solemn state,
To bless that lonely May-Flower,
  With all her Pilgrim-freight.

New-England's lofty mountains
  Bow low their leafy crest,
In homage to the swelling bay
  That gave the May-Flower rest,
In homage to the rugged rock
  That stretch'd a wintry hand,
And welcomed to its snow-clad breast
  The fathers of our land.

But thou, O Rock of Plymouth,
  Like him of old, who lent
To stranger and wayfaring men
  The shelter of his tent,
Saw not, beneath the homely garb,
  With clear, prophetic eyes,
Nor through the strangers' vestment scann'd
  The angel in disguise.

THE TULIP AND EGLANTINE.

THE Tulip call'd to the Eglantine :
  " Good neighbour, I hope you see
How the throngs that visit the garden come
  To pay their respects to me :
The florist admires my elegant robe,
  And praises its rainbow ray,
Till it seems as if through his raptured eyes
  He was gazing his soul away."

" It may be so," said the Eglantine ;
  " In a humble nook I dwell,
And what is passing among the great
  I cannot know so well ;
But they speak of me as the flower of Love,
  And that low, whisper'd name,
Is dearer to me and my infant buds
  Than the loudest breath of fame."

THE DYING MOTHER.

"How sweet to gaze upon thy placid brow,
My child! my child! like some unfolding bud
Of stainless snow-drop. Ah, how sweet to catch
Thy gentle breath upon my cheek, and feel
The bright redundance of thy silken hair,
My beautiful first-born. Life seems more fair
Since thou art mine. How soon amid its flowers
Thy little feet will gambol by my side,
My own pet-lamb. And then to train thee up
To be an angel, and to live for God—
O glorious hope!"

Fast fell the tears of joy
As the young mother spake.

But deep within,
A foe was busy at the seat of life,
And other language than her own fond hopes
Was traced by dire disease. A hollow voice
In midnight visions warn'd her of the tomb.
The surge roll'd heavy, yet there was a Rock
On which her soul found rest when the frail flesh
Wasted away.

"The cup my Father gives,
Shall I not drink it?"

So she bow'd her down,
While the new tie that bound her to the earth
So tenderly, was cut—then stretch'd her hand

To the Redeemer, whom in days of youth
She served and honour'd, and went home—*went home.*

—And now, Heaven bless thee, babe, whose tiny bark
Is launch'd so lonely on this tossing sea
Of time and change; and mid thy future course,
If here, in our dark clime, thy years unfold,
Bind her fair image to thy loving heart,
My little one, and let thy father hear
From thy young lips the same rejoicing words
Of piety and peace, which thrill'd his heart
With grateful prayer when at his fireside sat
The chosen idol of his early love.

THE TREE OF LOVE.

Beside the dear, domestic bower,
There sprang a tree of healing power;
Its leaflets, damp with gentle rain,
Could sooth or quell the pang of pain;
And 'neath its shade a maiden grew,
She shared its fruit, she drank its dew.

Oft at her side a youth was seen,
With glance of love and noble mien;
At twilight hour a favour'd guest,
Her trembling hand he warmly press'd;
At length, with guileless heart and free,
She said, "I'll plant that tree for thee."

Her little brother climb'd her knee:
"You must not go away from me;
The nightly prayer with me you say,
And sooth me when I'm tired of play:"
His sister's eye with tears was dim:
She said, "I'll plant that tree for him."

"Its roots are deep," the mother said;
"Beyond the darkling grave they spread:"
"Thy hand is weak," the father cried;
"Too young thou art to be a bride."
Serene she spake, "I look above
For strength to plant the tree of love."

Before the holy priest she stood,
Her fair cheek dy'd with rushing blood;
And as, with hands to heaven display'd,
Strong vows upon her soul he laid,
Her heaving breast, like fluttering bird,
Her snowy mantle wildly stirr'd.

But when the hallow'd cirque of gold,
Of deathless love the promise told,
Mysterious power her spirit felt,
And at the altar's foot she knelt:
"My God, my God, I'll cling to thee,
And plant for him that blessed tree."

Around their home its branches spread,
Its buds she nursed, its root she fed;
Though flaunting crowds, with giddy look,
Of toil so meek slight notice took,
Yet hovering angels mark'd with pride
The green tree of the blessed bride.

THE LAST SONG.

"SING to me love, thy voice is sweet!
It falls upon my ear
Like summer-gales o'er breathing flowers,
And makes even sickness dear;
Sing to me, love, the hour is meet,
This twilight hour serene,
Too dim to let officious care
Intrude high thoughts between.

Sing to me, love, the time is short,
I feel my strength decay,
The ties that bound my soul so fast
Melt like a dream away."
She sang to cheer his pensive mood
A deep and tuneful strain,
The changeless bliss of heaven how pure,
And earthly joys how vain.

At first, all tremulous and faint,
Awoke the warbling tone,
Then clearer, higher rose, and caught
An ardour not its own;
Strength, strength, as for an hour of need,
As if her lip were made
The harp on which some spirit-hand
Celestial measures play'd.

It ceased, and from the casement near
  The curtain's fold she drew,
And the young moon mid bowering leaves
  Look'd lone and peaceful through;
Where was the sigh of tender praise?
  Love's ne'er forgotten word?
Sleeps he? *How pale!* Alas, no breath
  Her sweeping tresses stirr'd.

A cry broke forth. He heeds it not!
  Young wife, thy lot was blest,
To charm the pang of mortal pain,
  And sing him to his rest;
Entranced the listening spirit soar'd
  Heavenward on balmy air,
And pass'd from love and music *here,*
  To love and music *there.*

THE MOURNER COMFORTED.

"My boy was beautiful, and he is dead!
Oh, speak no more to me. The voice of man
Grates on my ear, for I would be alone—
Alone, to weep."
Long flow'd that mourner's tears,
But then beside the Bible she knelt down,
And laid her cheek upon its hallow'd page,
And said, "God comfort me."
And as she closed
The fervent prayer, methought a still small voice
Bade the swoln surges of her soul be still,
That He who walk'd upon Tiberias' lake,
Ruling the midnight storm, might thither come,
And save from shipwreck.
Then, with pang subdued,
Her heart went wandering to her loved one's grave,
Marking in every bud that blossom'd there,
In every joyous butterfly that spread
Its radiant wing amid the flowers, a type
Of glorious resurrection. Every drop
Of dew that sparkled on the turf-clad mound
Seem'd holy to her. Even the bitter grief
That made the parting hour so desolate,
Put on the robe of humble faith, and said,
"'Tis well, my Lord, well with the little one
That dwells with thee."

And then methought she heard
A sound of heavenly harpings, and beheld
Celestial gleamings of cherubic wings,
And mid the song of ransom'd infancy
Unto its Saviour, caught the tuneful voice
Of her own cherish'd nursling.

So her lip
Join'd in deep praise. For how could she forbear
To thank her God for him who ne'er should taste
Of trouble more?

Was it his tender tone
That whisper'd, as she lay that night in dreams,
"Oh, mother, weep no more; but with a heart
Of holy love, hold on thy Christian path,
And come to me. For He who took on earth
Young children to his arms, will bid in heaven
The mother find her babe. So keep thine eye
Clear from the grief-cloud, for the time is short,
The way is plain: dear mother, come to me."

ART THOU A CHRISTIAN?

Art thou a Christian? Though thy cot
Be rude, and poverty thy lot,
A wealth is thine which earth denies,
A treasure boundless as the skies;
Gold and the diamond fade with shame,
Before thy casket's deathless flame;
Heir of high heaven! how canst thou sigh
For gilded dross and vanity?

Art thou a Christian, doom'd to roam
Far from thy friends and native home?
O'er trackless wilds uncheer'd to go,
With none to share an exile's wo?
Where'er thou find'st a Father's care,
Thy country and thy home are there:
How canst thou, then, a stranger be,
Surrounded by His family?

Art thou a Christian, mid the strife
Of years mature and burden'd life?
Thy heaven-born faith its shield shall spread
To guard thee in the hour of dread;
Thorns mid thy flinty path may spring,
Dire Pain inflict its scorpion sting,
But in thy soul a beacon-light
Shall guide thy pilgrim steps aright,
And balm from God's own fountain flow
To heal the wounds of earthly wo.

A NAME.

"Let us make us a name, lest we be scattered abroad."—*Genesis*, xi., 4.

Make to thyself a name,
  Not with a breath of clay,
Which, like the broken, hollow reed,
  Doth sigh itself away;
Not with the fame that vaunts
  The tyrant on his throne,
And hurls its stigma on the soul
  That God vouchsafes to own.

Make to thyself a name,
  Nor such as wealth can weave,
Whose warp is but a thread of gold,
  That dazzles to deceive;
Not with the tints of Love
  Form out its letters fair,
That scroll within thy hand shall fade
  Like him who placed it there.

Make to thyself a name,
  Not in the sculptured aisle,
The marble oft betrays its trust,
  Like Egypt's lofty pile;
But ask of Him who quell'd
  Of death, the victor-strife,
To write it on the blood-bought page
  Of everlasting life.

LAST WORDS OF AN INDIAN CHIEF.

"He cometh! Death is here. Leave me alone!
Hence! hence! Ye shall not see me when I die,
If die I must. I would not that the men
Whom I have led to battle saw me yield
To any conqueror. Shall my warriors hear
From this undaunted breast the gasp or groan
As when a woman dies?

"How cold the dew
Starts o'er my temples! Wipe it not away.
Shame on your tears! Leave me alone with Death!
For I will meet him as a brave man should,
And hurl defiance at him.

"What is this?
Ha! He hath smote the lion! Was it well
To steal upon me in my unarm'd bed,
Most potent enemy? How hast thou cut
The nerve of that strong arm, which used to cleave
The proudest foeman like the sapling spray!
Oh friends! the dimness of the grave doth steal
Over those eyes, that as the eagle dared
The noontide sunbeam. Let me hear your voice
Once more! once more!

"In vain! The ear is seal'd
Which caught the rustle of the lightest leaf
Where the close ambush lay. Come back! come back!
Hear my last bidding, friends! Lay not my bones

Near any white man's bones. Let not his hand
Touch my clay pillow, nor his hateful voice
Sing burial hymns for me. Rather than dwell
In Paradise with him, my soul would choose
Eternal darkness and the undying worm.
Ho! heed my words, or else my wandering shade
Shall haunt ye with its curse!"

And so he died,
That pagan chief; the last strong banner-staff
Of the poor Senecas. No more the flash
Of his wild eloquence shall fire their ranks
To mortal combat. His distorted brow,
And the stern grapple when he sank in death,
Sadly they grave upon their orphan hearts,
As to their rude homes in the forest glade
Mournful they turn'd.

SLEEPING CHILD.

Sleep, dearest, long and sweet,
  With smile upon thy brow,
Thy restless, tottering feet
  Are surely weary now,
Trotting about all day
  Upon the nursery-floor,
Or happier still to play
Among the wild-flowers gay
  Beside thy father's door.

Thy little laughing eyes,
  How tranquilly they rest,
Thy tiny fingers clasp'd
  Upon thy guiltless breast,
While o'er thy placid face
  The stealing moonbeams fall,
And with a heaven-taught grace
Thy baby features trace
  Upon the shaded wall.

Sleep, dearest! She whose ear
  Her nursing-infant's sigh
Hath never waked to hear
  When midnight's hush was nigh,

Ne'er felt its balmy kiss
  The cradle-care repay,
Hath she not chanced to miss
The deepest, purest bliss
  That cheers life's pilgrim-way?

To see each budding power
  Thy Maker's goodness bless,
To catch the manna-shower
  Of thy full tenderness,
The immortal mind to train—
  No more divine employ
Thy mother seeks to gain,
Until her spirit drain
  The seraph cup of joy.

GEMINI.

TWINS of the heavenly house, how fair
Your guerdons to our planet are!
  Skies ye paint of richest blue,
And where the daisy's eye is found
Peeping from the moisten'd ground,
  Ye lead those crystal waters through
Which old Aquarius bound.
The winged tenants of the grove
Greet ye with a song of love,
As mid the green boughs, void of fear,
Their chambers soft and warm they rear:
Hovers round each blooming stalk
  The bee, with nectar fill'd,
And ants within the garden walk
  Their cone-roof'd cities build.

Sounds from every rippling shore
Speak the reign of winter o'er,
Shouting boys, with mirthful note,
Gayly launch the tiny boat,
And the new-fledged ducklings play
On their oary-footed way,
And when Evening dims the lake,
Frogs their hoarse orchestra wake,
And the tortoise loves to tell,
Peering from his mottled shell,

'Tween the water and the land,
Tales his comrades understand.

Starry twins! your earliest ray
  England's merry rustics hail,
Round the Maypole circling gay
  In the primrose-scented vale.
Every cottage sends its pride,
Youth, or maid, or recent bride,
  To the thronging village plain,
While the matron, mid her care,
In her daughter's beauty rare,
  Lives her triumphs o'er again.
E'en that much-enduring race,*
Who upon the darken'd face
Bear the symbol of their state,
Outcast and unfortunate,
Seem to hope and freedom born
On young May's propitious morn,
And throughout the toil-worn year,
Climbing high in chimney drear,
Guard the memory, sadly gay,
Of their lonely holyday.

Ancient Rome, with festive rite,
Hailed ye, glittering twins of light,
And the wreaths of Flora cast,
Where your blended footsteps past.
Classic Greece, with legends hoar,
Link'd her lineage to your lore,

* The chimney-sweep boys, who in London have their holyday on the first of May.

Pointing with her haughty hand
To the Argonautic band,
Who to win the fleece of gold
Dared the seas with Jason bold.

But from your refulgent urn
To a higher source we turn;
To Him who, with a shepherd's care,
Arcturus feeds in fields of air,
Rules Orion's wrath, and sees
The duly marshall'd Pleiades.
Hath He not the zodiac's bound
Traced these azure skies around?
Bidding every season prove
Changeless, unforgetful love,
That by teachers so divine,
Starry lessons, line on line,
Man, the pupil of the sky,
  Might be taught with praise to glow,
And the love that lights his eye,
  To his brother's heart to show?

TO A FRAGMENT OF COTTON.

Methinks thou'rt indestructible. At first
But the slight remnant of a spruce cravat,
Thou cam'st unbidden to my premises,
And then the baby tore thee, and the dog
Did munch thee in a corner, where he play'd ;
Next thou wert hanging at the housemaid's broom,
Yet here thou art, for all.
Hast e'er a tongue?
No doubt. The veriest triflers oft can boast
Great store of words. If thou hast aught to say,
I'll be a listener. Tell me of thy birth,
And all thy strange mutations, since the dow
Of infancy was on thee, to thine hour
Of finish'd beauty 'neath the shuttle's skill.

So, thou wert known in history ! and thy sire
The sounding name of Sir Gossypium bore.
He was a younger brother of the fleece,
And of the flax of Egypt, and the silk
Which the poor spinning-worm doth die to make
A present of, to those who thank her not.
Thy race have multiplied exceedingly,
And sown themselves in every sunny zone
Of both the hemispheres. The planter's hand,
Well pleased, doth play about their thickening beard
When its young promise tints the ripen'd cheek.

Thy name is mention'd where the merchants meet,
And Commerce loves thee well. Yea, thou dost make
Much clamour in the world, with thundering crash
Of water-wheel, and loom, and steaming smoke
From coal-fed chimneys, fusing to the skies
With blacken'd breath. Yet mid thy vassal throng
Of toiling artisans, 'tis sad to see
Such troops of little ones, with pallid cheek,
Yielding their joyous birthright at thy shrine,
And all sweet intercourse with fields and flowers,
That glads the peasant's child.
'Twere hard to count
Thy many transmigrations, or to keep
Tithe of the dramas where thou dost enact
Most changeful parts. Thou in the vessel's hold
Dost slumber heavily, in ponderous bales,
Like precious ingots, or with winged sail
Impel its trackless journey o'er the deep,
Or, closely furl'd, embrace the groaning mast
That crouches to the tempest. Thou dost stoop,
With garment coarse, to wrap the labouring kind,
And deck the country-dame in Sunday-gown
Of ample-flower'd and many-colour'd chints,
Or, slow emerging from the Indian loom,
Light as the texture of a dreamy thought,
Veil the fair bride, and drape the throned queen.
With man thou art when to the dust he goes,
And in thy snowy shroud dost fold his brow
When friend and lover have forsaken him.

But yet thou hast a higher ministry
Of kindliness, and, when thou well hast served

His body's need, dost turn thy hand and touch
The ethereal mind. Yea, when thou seem'st to die,
Thou only dropp'st thy grosser elements
To commune with the soul.

Mysterious Guest!
I seem to fear thee. Would that I had known
Thy lineage better, and been less remiss
In the good grace of hospitality.
I much bemoan myself that thou shouldst be
So treated in my house. With reverent hand
And genuflection, I do take thee up,
And straight bespeak for thee more fitting place
Mid thy compeers.

But who can say what form
Thou next may'st wear?

Perchance the pictured page
Through which the lisping and delighted child
Hath its first talk with knowledge, or the chart
That saves the mariner mid rocks and shoals
Upon the wrecking sea.

Or lov'st thou best
To be the tablet of the sage? or bear
The bard's rich music to another age?
Or with some message from the Book of Life,
Wake the dead slumber of benighted lands?

THE BEAUTIFUL CHILD.

Fair child, whose gem of genius burn'd
In beauty's purest gold enshrined,
On whom the eye of strangers turn'd
With wonder and delight combined,

Whose tender, tuneful voice doth keep
Fresh echo while long seasons roll,
As music, though the lute-strings sleep,
Still lingereth in the master's soul,

We will not say how early fled!
Nor, darkly murmuring, mark thy date,
Though Grief's most bitter tear be shed,
And home's fond temple desolate;

For life is long that fills the round
Which Heaven's own finger brightly traced,
And many a form that age hath crown'd
Must leave that circle unembraced.

But thine eternal life, how blest!
O let its radiant image be
A watch-light in the parents' breast,
Till joyful they ascend to thee.

THE THREE LITTLE GRAVES.

I SOUGHT at twilight's pensive hour
  The path which mourners tread,
Where many a marble fane reveals
  The City of the Dead;
The City of the Dead, where all
  From feverish toil repose,
While round their homes the simple flower
  In sweet profusion blows.

And there I mark'd a pleasant spot,
  Enclosed with tender care,
Where, side by side, three infants lay,
  The only tenants there;
Nor weed nor bramble raised its head
  To mar the hallow'd scene,
And doubtless 'twas a mother's tear
  That kept the turf so green.

The eldest was a gentle girl,
  She sank as rose-buds fall,
And then her baby brothers came,
  They were their parents' all.
Their parents' all! Ah! think how deep
  The wail of sickness rose,
Ere, 'neath these solitary mounds,
  They found a long repose.

Their cradle-sports beside the hearth,
  At winter's eve, are o'er,
Their tuneful tones, so full of mirth,
  Delight the ear no more ;
Yet still their thrilling memory lives,
  And many a lisping sound,
And sweetly broken phrase doth steal
  The sorrowing heart around.

Three little graves ! Three little graves !
  Come hither, ye who see
Your blooming babes around you smile,
  A blissful company,
And of those childless mourners think
  With sympathizing pain,
And sooth them with a Saviour's words,
  "Your dead shall rise again."

R

TO A GOOSE.

I CANNOT bear to hear thee slander'd, Goose!
It irketh me to see the truant boys
Pause in their play, and cast a stone at thee,
And call thee foolish.
                                        Do those worthies know
That when old Rome had let the ruffian Gauls
Tread on her threshold of vitality,
And all her sentinels were comatose,
Thy charion-call did save her? Mighty strange
To call *thee* fool!
                                        I think thou'rt dignified
And portly in thy bearing, and in all
The duties and proprieties of life
Art quite a pattern. Yet the duck may quack,
The turkey gabble, and the guinea-hen
Keep up a piercing and perpetual scream,
And all is well; but if thou ope thy beak,
"*Fie, silly creature!*"
                                        Yet I'm sure thou'st done
Many a clever and obliging deed;
And more than this, thou from thy wing dost spare
An outcast feather, which hath woke the world,
And made it wiser.
                                        Yea, the modest quill
Doth take its quiet stand behind the press,
And, like a prompter, tell it what to say.

But yet we never praise the goose, who gave
This precious gift. Yet what can fill its place?
Think of the clumsy stylus, how absurd!
I know, indeed, that smart metallic pens
Have undertook to speculate at large,
But I eschew them all, and prophesy
Goose-quills will be immortal, as the art
To which they minister. 'Twere meet for me,
Though all beside were dumb, to fondly laud
The instrument that from my childhood up
Hath been my solace and my chosen friend
In hours of loneliness.
I'd fain propose
That, mid the poultry in the farmer's yard,
The goose should wear a ducal coronet.
But our republic would not authorize
Aught like an order of nobility;
And so I institute a simple claim
For justice long withheld. I ask my peers,
The erudite and learned in the law,
Why the recusant owl is singled out
As Wisdom's bird? If blind Mythology,
Who on her fingers scarcely knew to count
Her thirty thousand gods, should groping make
Such error, 'tis not strange. But we, who skill
To ride the steam, and have a goodly hope
To ride the lightning too, need we be ruled
By vacillating Delphos? or stand still
To sanction her mistakes?
The aforesaid owl,
With his dull, staring eyes, what hath he done
To benefit mankind? Moping all day

Amid some dodder'd oak, and then at night,
With hideous hooting and wild flapping wings,
Scaring the innocent child. What hath he done
To earn a penny, or to make the world
Richer in any way? I doubt if he
Even gets an honest living. Who can say
Whether such midnight rambles, none know where,
Are for his credit? Yet the priceless crown
Of wisdom he in symbol and in song
Unrighteously hath worn.

But times have changed,
Most reverend owl! Utility bears rule,
And the shrewd spirit of a busy age
Dotes not on things antique, nor pays respect
To hoary hairs, but counts it loss of time
To honour whatsoever fails to yield
A fat per centage. Yet thou'rt not ashamed
To live a gentleman, nor bronze thy claw
With manual labour, stupidly content
To be a burden on community.

—Meantime, the worthy and hard-working goose
Hath rear'd us goslings, fed us with her flesh,
Lull'd us to sleep upon her softest down,
And with her quills maintain'd the lover's lore,
And saved the tinsel of the poet's brain.
—Dear goose, thou'rt greatly wrong'd.

I move the owl
Be straightway taken from the usurper's seat,
And thou forthwith be voted for, to fill
Minerva's arms.

The flourish of a pen

Hath saved or lost a realm, hath sign'd the bond
That made the poor man rich—reft from the prince
His confiscated wealth, and sent him forth
A powerless exile—for the prisoner bade
The sunbeam tremble through his iron bars
The last, last time—or changed the cry of war
To blessed peace.
And yet we scorn the bird
Whose cast-off feather hath done this, and more.

ON HEARING SACRED MUSIC WELL PERFORMED.

ADDRESSED TO A YOUNG LADY.

CAME they, in vision to thy soul,
They who the harps of heaven control,
What time in infant slumbers thrown,
The unform'd mind receives its tone?
Drank *then* thy tuneful lips their sigh
Of deep, entrancing harmony,
Unconscious of the balm it drew,
Like rose-bud bathed in Hermon's dew?

—Or dwell'st thou to their hymning sphere,
Than we of grosser clay, more near?
Inhaling that ethereal note
Which on some lucid cloud may float,
And wooing thence the warbled air,
To cheat us of our earthly care?

—When thou to them at last shalt soar,
Bright pupil of seraphic lore,
No strange or occult thing to thee,
The language of the skies must be,
Who scann'd on earth its melody.

SONNET.

Pride, take thy mingled cup. The treacherous world
Hath dregg'd it for thee, though her smile was bright;
Yea, when her lip with promised joy was curl'd,
She falsely mingled myrrh and aconite;

And mid thy revels in thy lofty halls,
A sever'd hand, with fingers pale and still,
Wrote "Mene—Mene—Tekel" on thy walls,
But yet repine not, thou hast had thy will;

The sparkling foam, from earth's enchantments born,
Didst thou not choose it for thy daily draught?
And didst thou not the poor in spirit scorn,
Who with unswerving step and chasten'd thought

Held on the "narrow way," mid rock and thorn,
And duly bow'd the knee unto the manger-born?

THE NEW-ENGLAND VILLAGE.

VERDANT and beautiful! How fair thy vales!
With what a smile thy gentle river glides,
While through the vale of interwoven boughs
Thy peaceful dwellings pleasantly look forth.
Yon hallow'd temple, crown'd with snowy spire,
Casts a lone shadow o'er the sacred spot
Where sleeps the white-hair'd shepherd mid his flock,
The loved of God and man. The statesman's head,
With all its gather'd mass of curious lore,
Lock'd up in marble; and the soldier's arm,
Strong for his country in her hour of need,
Are here, too, 'neath the turf. And there, amid
The lawns and gardens which their hands had dress'd,
The ancient fathers, with their numerous race,
Securely dwelt.
Yon mansion hath a voice
Of other days. Through the dim lapse of years
And rule of strangers, still around its halls
Flit cherish'd images of good old times,
When hospitality, with grasp sincere,
Led to her board the unexpected guest,
And, careless of the pomp of proud array
Or servitude of menials, warm'd the heart
To social joy.
I do remember, too,
How in my early years yon dome sent forth

The daughter in her bridal loveliness,
To wreathe fresh roses round a distant home,
And stately sons, all strong and bold, to take
Their untried portion in this tossing world.
From thence the father to an honour'd grave
Was borne; and there the mother of the flock,
Lovely and loved as in her day of bloom,
Sank meekly on her couch to rise no more:
And the sweet haunts of her sweet ministry
Have lost her name forever. Yet the vine
That gadding round her nursery-window climb'd,
Still lives unnurtured; and methinks its leaves
Thrill with the lore of hoarded memories,
Pleasant, yet mournful.

But that ancient race,
With whom our heart's deep reverence dwelt so long,
Methinks at such an hour they seem to stand
Again among us, even more palpably
Than those we call the living. Wait we not
At hush of eve for them? dreaming we hear
Their footsteps in the rustle of the leaves,
Or their low whisper, warning us to seek
A home not made with hands?

So may it be;
And to that home eternal every one
Who here were rapt in the frank fellowship
Of simpler days, and mourn its loss with tears,
Be gather'd, where no more the blight of ill,
Or fear of change, or sigh of pain shall steal
O'er the pure mingling of congenial souls.

LAURA BRIDGMAN,

THE DEAF, DUMB, AND BLIND GIRL, AT THE INSTITUTION FOR THE BLIND IN BOSTON.

WHERE is the light that to the eye
  Heaven's holy message gave,
Tinging the retina with rays
  From sky, and earth, and wave?

Where is the sound that to the soul
  Mysterious passage wrought,
And strangely made the moving lip
  A harp-string for the thought?

All fled! all lost! Not even the rose
  An odour leaves behind,
That, like a broken reed, might trace
  The tablet of the mind.

That mind! It struggles with its fate,
  The anxious conflict, see!
As if through Bastile-bars it sought
  Communion with the free.

Yet still its prison-robe it wears
  Without a prisoner's pain,
For happy childhood's beaming sun
  Glows in each bounding vein.

And bless'd Philosophy is near,
  In Christian armour bright,
To scan the subtlest clew that leads
  To intellectual light.

Say, lurks there not some ray of heaven
  Amid thy bosom's night,
Some echo from a better land,
  To make the smile so bright?

The lonely lamp in Greenland cell,
  Deep 'neath a world of snow,
Doth cheer the loving household group
  Though none beside may know;

And, sweet one, doth our Father's hand
  Place in thy casket dim
A radiant and peculiar lamp,
  To guide thy steps to Him?

DEATH OF A FRIEND.

It is not when the good obey
  The summons of their God,
And meekly take the narrow couch
  Beneath the burial sod,
That keenest anguish pours its wail,
  Despairing o'er their rest,
For praise should mingle with the pang
  That wrings the mourner's breast.

It is not when the saint departs,
  Whose wealth was hid on high,
That bitterest tears of grief should gush
  From sad bereavement's eye;
For in the consummation blest
  Of every wish and prayer,
He to his Father's courts ascends,
  And finds a mansion there.

But yet, oh friend, revered and blest,
  Who from our arms this day
Hast risen to gain thy perfect rest
  In realms of cloudless day,
Though faith reveals thee to our view
  From every sorrow free,
How shall we check the bursting tear
  That wildly flows for thee?

Self-sacrificing, upright, pure,
  Of feeble hope the guide,
With judgment clear, a soul subdued,
  And wealth without its pride,
The widow in her lowly cell
  Must long thy loss deplore,
The orphans wait thy step in vain,
  Thou com'st to them no more.

The path of duty and of zeal,
  Who now, like thee, shalt tread?
And deeply for ourselves we mourn
  That thou art of the dead.

S

TRUE WISDOM.

"So teach us to number our days, that we may apply our hearts unto wisdom."—David.

Why break the limits of permitted thought
To revel in Elysium? thou who bear'st
Still the stern yoke of this unresting life,
Its toils, its hazards, and its fears of change?
Why hang thy frostwork wreath on Fancy's brow,
When Labour warns thee to thy daily task,
And Faith doth bid thee gird thyself to run
A faithful journey to the gate of Heaven?

Up, 'tis no dreaming-time! awake! awake!
For He who sits on the High Judge's seat
Doth in his record note each wasted hour,
Each idle word. Take heed thy shrinking soul
Find not their weight too heavy when it stands
At that dread bar from whence is no appeal.
For while we trifle the light sand steals on,
Leaving the hour-glass empty. So thy life
Glideth away. Stamp wisdom on its hours.

THE MOTHER SUMMONED.

"The feast of life is sweet,
I am no weary guest,
Loving friends my presence greet,
And all that charms the eye or ear,
Taste to please, or heart to cheer,
Earth, sky, and ocean gather here—
God's care be blest.

'Tis scarce the hour of prime,
But how the sands of Time
Steal fast away!
Yet till cool evening falls
With lamplight on the walls—
I fain would stay.

If this be long and late,
Oh Thou! who mark'st our date,
Till twilight's ray
I'd love to linger here,
Guiding my children dear
Their pilgrim-way;

Watching their minds unfold,
Rich with unrusting gold
Of knowledge stored,
Till each his manly seat
Shall take, in concord sweet,
Around life's board."

The Master call'd ! the mother heard :
" *Come hither !*" was the solemn word.
Bright shone the noonday sun,
The undrain'd cup still glow'd with sparkling zest,
She clasp'd her pure hands o'er her breast,
" *Thy will be done.*"

In the fresh summer of her years
She kiss'd away her nursling's tears,
And laid him, lull'd to quiet rest,
Upon her blooming daughter's breast.

Pain probed her nerves to Torture's pang,
The fibrous heart-strings rent and rang,
Yet peace, that of her soul was part,
Look'd through her eye, and foil'd the dart
That rankled there,
And Faith the Saviour's image drew,
Wiping away the deathful dew
With words of prayer.

On a high arm and strong,
Her soul its burden cast,
While soaring, soaring high,
The weakness of mortality
Fell like a dried leaf on the blast,
And with a conqueror's song
Heaven's gate she pass'd.

PARTING.

Not of the boisterous wave,
  Not of the tempest's power,
Not of the rent and cleaving bark,
  Speak at this sacred hour.

God of the trusting soul!
  God of the traveller, hear!
And from our parting cup of love
  Wring out these dregs of fear.

Art thou a God at home,
  Where the bright fireside smiles,
And not abroad, upon the deep,
  Mid danger's deadliest wiles?

What though the eyes so dear
  To distant regions turn,
Their tender language in our hearts
  Like vestal flame shall burn.

What though the voice beloved
  Respond not to our pain,
We'll shut its music in the soul
  Until we meet again.

Farewell! we're travellers all,
  With one bless'd goal in view,
One rest, one everlasting home,
  Sweet friend, a sweet adieu!

THE DEEP.

I FAIN would be thy pupil, mighty Deep!
Yet speak thou gently to me, for I fear
Thy lifted terror, and I would not learn
The lesson that doth make the mariner
So deadly pale.
                                My mother Earth doth teach
An easy lore. She likes to speak of man.
Her levell'd mountains and her cultured vales,
Town, tower, and temple, and triumphal arch,
All speak of man, and moulder while they speak.
But of whose architecture and design
Tell thine eternal fountains, when they rise
To combat with the clouds, or when they fall?
Of whose strong culture speak thy sunless plants,
And groves and gardens, which no mortal eye
Hath seen and lived?
                                What sculptor's art hath wrought
Those coral monuments and tombs of pearl,
Where sleeps the sea-boy, mid a pomp that earth
Denies her buried kings?
                                Whose science stretch'd
The simplest line to curb thy monstrous tide,
And, writing "*Hitherto*" upon the sand,
Bade thy mad surge respect it?
                                From whose loom
Comes forth thy drapery, that ne'er waxeth old?

Who hath thy keys, thou deep? Who taketh note
Of all thy wealth? Who numbereth the host
That make their bed with thee? What eye doth scan
Thy secret annal, from creation lock'd
Fast in those dark, illimitable cells,
Which he who visited hath ne'er return'd
To commune with the living?
One reply!
Do all thine echoing depths and tossing waves
Make but one answer? of that One Dread Name
Which he who deepest graves within his heart
Is wisest, though the world may call him fool?

Therefore I come, a listener to thy voice,
And bow me at thy feet, and touch my lip
To thy cool billow, if perchance my soul,
That fleeting wanderer on these shores of time,
May, by thy voice instructed, learn of God.

PLANTING FLOWERS ON THE GRAVE OF PARENTS.

I'VE set the flow'rets where ye sleep,
  Father and mother dear,
Their roots are in the mould so deep,
  Their bosoms bear a tear;
The tear-drop of the dewy morn
  Their trembling casket fills,
Mix'd with that essence from the heart
  Which filial love distils.

Above thy pillow, mother dear,
  I've placed thy favourite flower,
The bright-eyed purple violet,
  That deck'd thy summer-bower;
The fragrant chamomile, that spreads
  Its verdure fresh and green,
And richly broiders every niche
  The velvet turf between.

I kiss'd the tender violet
  That droop'd its stranger-head,
And call'd it blessed thus to grow
  So near my precious dead;
And when my venturous path shall be
  Across the deep blue sea,
I bade it in its beauty rise,
  And guard that spot for me.

There was no other child, my dead!
  To do this deed for thee;
Mother! no other nursling babe
  E'er sat upon thy knee,
And, father! that endearing name,
  No other lips than mine
E'er breathed to prompt thy hallow'd prayer
  At morn or eve's decline.

Tear not those flowers, thou idle child,
  Tear not the flowers that wave
In sweet and simple sanctity
  Around this humble grave,
Lest guardian angels from the skies,
  That watch amid the gloom,
Should dart reproachful ire on those
  Who desecrate the tomb.

And spare to pluck my sacred plants,
  Ye groups that wander nigh,
When summer sunsets fire with gold
  The glorious western sky,
That, when your sleep is in the dust,
  Where now your footsteps tread,
Some kindred hand may train the rose
  To grace your lowly bed.

"LORD, REMEMBER US."

St. Luke.

Behold the babe, with ceaseless cry,
Just entering on mortality.
Oh Saviour! thou for whom wert spread,
Mid wondering brutes, the manger-bed,
With pity view its feeble strife,
And fan the trembling spark of life.

The boy, with giddy footsteps, strays
Through hidden Danger's devious maze;
Thou! who in childhood's wayward hour,
Wert subject to thy mother's power,
Withdraw his heart from Folly's snare,
And in Thy wisdom let him share.

The man mature, mid noontide heat,
Temptation's countless forms must meet;
Redeemer! thou who scorn and care
With meek, unanswering love didst bear,
His burdens ease, his thoughts control,
And with thy patience arm his soul.

The lonely stranger sorrowing roves,
An exile from the land he loves;
Thou, who but in one cottage glade
At Bethany wert welcome made,
Speak peace when deep despondence sighs,
And tell of mansions in the skies.

The mourner droops with heaving breast,
Low, where his buried idols rest;
Remember, Thou, who once didst shed
The tear of grief o'er friendship's bed,
Remember! let thy mercy flow,
And bless for heaven those pangs of wo.

The death-struck, on his couch of pain,
Feels every earthly solace vain;
The eye is glazed, the spirit faint,
Redeemer! cheer thy suffering saint;
Infuse thy strength when nature dies,
And to thy presence bid him rise.

LIBRARY OF DR. BOWDITCH.

"It is our hope and expectation, that for many years this apartment will remain as it was left."—*Memoir by his Son.*

Yes, leave it as it was, untouch'd, unchanged,
And consecrate to hallow'd memories
Of him, the clear-soul'd man, who dwelt with truth
As with a brother.

Break not their array,
Those sages and philosophers, who mix'd
Their thoughts with his, feeding the altar-flame
Of science, with fresh incense day and night.
Spake not the voices of the solemn stars
Here to their votary? Scann'd they here, his eye
Unwearied, searching out their mystic laws?
And shed they not, from their eternal lamps,
Serener light on him?

Methinks 'twere sin
To pry with curious or irreverent hand
Amid those pages where his self-taught mind
Imbodied its creations. O'er yon desk
How oft he toil'd amid the tomes he loved,
To make the occult luminous, and strew
The priceless jewels of profoundest thought
To the wayfaring man, or him who steers
With naught but seas around and skies above—
The hardy mariner.

T

Move not the chair
Where by his side *she* sat, the tenderest friend,
The mother of his children, her fond glance
Intently resting on his studious brow,
And oft by looks of answering love repaid.
Here, too, his little ones, fearing no chill
Of pedant frown, came flocking, for he join'd
Their happy sports with full hilarity.
—How bright his image, in this favour'd spot,
Gleams o'er the sorrowing friend. Here was his wont
To pour the tides of healthful feeling forth,
In social interchange; for still with him
Majestic Science, in her loftiest heights,
Knew no austerity, but hand in hand
Walk'd with life's charities.
And thus he lived,
And thus, with cheerful acquiescence, met
His euthanasia, and lay down in peace,
His couch of pain made soft by filial hands.

—Then let this haunt be sacred.
For the foot
Of strangers here in future days shall turn,
As to some Mecca of Philosophy;
And hither, too, the aspiring youth shall come
To question of his greatness, or to seek
Some relic of the wondrous man, whose fame
Still gathereth greenness from the hand of Time.

THE SAILOR'S APPEAL.

Ye dwellers on the stable land,
 Of danger what know ye,
Like us who brave the whelming surge,
 Or trust the treacherous sea?
The fair trees shade you from the sun,
 You see the harvests grow,
And breathe the fragrance of the breeze
 When the first roses blow.

You slumber on your beds of down,
 Close wrapp'd, in chambers warm,
Lull'd only to a deeper dream
 By the descending storm;
While high amid the slippery shroud
 We make our midnight path,
And e'en the strongest mast is bow'd
 Beneath the tempest's wrath.

Yet still, what know ye of the joy
 That lights our ocean-strife,
When on its way our gallant ship
 Rides like a thing of life;
When gayly towards the wish'd-for port
 With favouring wind we stand,
Or first your misty line descry,
 Hills of our native land!

There's deadly peril in our path
Beyond the wrecking blast,
A peril that may reach the soul
When life's short voyage is past;
Send us your Bibles when we go
To dare the whelming wave,
Your men of prayer, to teach us how
To meet a watery grave.

And, Saviour! thou whose foot sublime
The foaming surge did tread,
Whose hand the rash disciple drew
From darkness and the dead,
Oh! be our Ark when floods descend,
When thunders shake the spheres,
Our Ararat when tempests end,
And the green earth appears.

MORN AND EVEN.

"Thou makest the outgoings of the morning and of the evening to rejoice."—*David.*

The outgoings of sweet morn! See the light mist,
That spreads its white wing to the heavens away;
See the fresh blossoms by the blithe bee kiss'd;
The hilltop kindling 'neath the King of Day;
Spire after spire, that drinks the genial ray;
The rocks, that in their rifted holds abide,
And darkly frown, with heads forever gray;
While the clear stream gleams out in trembling pride
Through its transparent veil, like a fair, timid bride.

Morn to the Earth! the cup of life she quaffs,
And countless voices hail the sparkling draught,
Methinks the lamb beside its mother laughs;
Up soars the lark, with song his Maker taught;
Sweet lisping murmurs wrap the infant's thought,
As gladly from the cottage door it creeps;
The wild rill glitters through the lonely grot;
While the hoarse sea, whose anthem never sleeps,
Reverberates God's praise through all its sounding deeps.

Morn to the watcher by the sick man's bed!
The slow, slow clock tells out the welcome hour,
And to the air he springs with buoyant tread;
The poor caged bird sings sweet in lady's bower;

The farmer, watchful lest the skies may lower,
  Thrusts his sharp sickle mid the bearded grain;
While sportive voices, strong in childhood's power,
  With merry music wake the village plain,
And toil comes forth refresh'd, and age is young again.

The outgoings of mild eve! the folded rose;
  Soft slumber settling on the lily's bell;
The solemn forest lull'd to deep repose,
  While restless winds no more its murmurs swell;
The stars emerging from their secret cell,
  A silent night-watch o'er the world to keep;
And then the queenly moon, attended well,
  Who o'er the mighty arch of heaven doth sweep,
Speaking of Nature's King in language still and deep.

The charms of eve how sweet, he best can say,
  Who, sickening at the city's dust and noise,
And selfish arts that Mammon's votaries sway,
  Turns to his home to taste its simple joys;
There, climbing on his knee, his ruddy boys
  Wake that warm thrill which every care repays,
And fondly hasting from her baby-toys,
  His prattling daughter seeks a father's gaze,
And gives that tender smile which o'er his slumber plays.

She, too, who wins her bread by toil severe,
  And from her home at early morn must go
To earn the bread that dries her children's tear,
  How hails her heart, the sun declining low!
Love nerves the foot that else were sad and slow,
  And when afar her lowly roof she spies,
Forgot is all her lot of scorn and wo;

A mother's rapture kindles in her eyes,
As to her wearied arms the eager nursling flies.

And see, from labour loosed, the drooping team,
Unharness'd, hasting to their fragrant food,
While, fearful of the hawk's marauding scream,
The broad-wing'd mother folds her helpless brood;
In the cool chambers of the teeming flood
The scaly monsters check their boisterous play,
And, closely curtain'd mid the quiet wood,
The slumbering songsters hush their warbling lay,
While man's sweet hymn of praise doth close the summer
day.

BABE DYING IN ITS MOTHER'S ABSENCE.

He lay 'tween life and death.
The priestly hand
Shed the baptismal water on his brow,
While earnestly a solemn tone besought
A heavenly place for that departing soul,
In Jesus' name.
The eye lay heavily
And lustreless beneath the half-closed lids,
But the small fingers all spasmodic thrill'd
Within the nurse's clasp.
She was not there
Who nurtured that fair boy, and day by day
Mark'd his smooth limbs to fuller roundness grow,
And garner'd up each ringing, gleeful shout,
Like music in her heart. She was not there.
Had she but known his peril, what could stay
The rushing traveller? Not the mountains steep,
Nor swollen floods, nor midnight's blackest shade,
Nor wildest storm. Or had one darken'd dream,
Mid her fond intercourse with joyous friends,
Bore his changed image, not with sport and smile,
But sleepless, starting from his fever'd bed,
The pearly teeth gnash'd strongly, and the tongue,
Untrain'd to language, moaning out his grief;
Or had she seen him from his favourite cup
Still force the spoon away, till his fair lip,
So like a rosebud, sallow grew, and thin,

How had she burst away to see him die,
Or die with him.
But ah, too late! too late!
One bitter gasp upon a hireling's breast,
And all is o'er! Methought some lingering tie
Held him to earth. What did thy pale hand seek
With such a quivering eagerness, poor babe?
Thine absent mother? Didst thou long to feel
Her kiss upon thine eyelids, or her breath
Parting the curls, and passing up to heaven
A winged prayer?
Would that I could forget
The weeping of that mother, when she takes
That ice-cold body to her bursting heart;
Or even for that, too late, doth frantic press
The pitying sexton for one last, drear sight
Of her lost darling, in his desolate couch
Most desolate, amid the mouldering dead.

Mothers! who, bending o'er your cradled charge,
Feel an unspoken love, cling to his side
As the soul weds the clay. Can the whole earth,
With all its pageantry, the wandering glance
Scanning its proudest climes, buy one blest hour
Like his confiding slumber in your arms?
Ye answer, No.
So take your priceless meed,
The first young love of innocence, the smile
Singling you out from all the world beside;
And if, amid this hallow'd ministry,
Heaven's messenger should claim the unstain'd soul,
Yours be the hand to give it back to God.

THE GREENLAND CONVERT.

MID-WINTER in the arctic zone,
  On Greenland's sterile shore,
The frozen bay forgets to moan,
  Though wildest tempests roar;
No morn the shuddering skies to cheer,
  No sun the noon to light,
Unpitying darkness, long and drear,
  Commingleth day with night.

Close in each subterranean cell
  The shivering tenants clung,
While snows on snows incessant fell,
  And whirlwind banners swung;
Around the seal-fed lamp they drew,
  That spark of life to fan,
Which gleam'd with feeble radiance through
  Those effigies of man.

Keen frosts, like subtle serpents, stole
  To every secret nook,
And from the pulses of the soul
  Their lingering fervour took.
Dire sounds! the fearful icebergs quake,
  The solid rocks are riven,
As though opposing thunders spake
  Harsh words of war in heaven.

Oppress'd by sorrow's hopeless ban,
In this most dreary place
There dwelt a desolated man,
The last of all his race;
One daughter, when the rest were dead,
Long with her loving tone
Sustain'd his heart, but she had fled,
And he was left alone.

"Beata! in the blissful clime
Where now thy lot is cast,
Doth the young floweret reach its prime
Unsmitten by the blast?
Is there a sky without a cloud?
An undeclining day?
No famine-pang? no icy shroud?
My angel-daughter, say!

Oh, speak once more, with one sweet tone
Confirm the promise blest,
Whose spirit hush'd the parting groan
When thou didst sink to rest:"
Thus rose amid the rayless gloom
Poor Agusina's moan,
As with his lost one in the tomb
He held communion lone.

Oft, in the sacred Book of God,
With tearful toil he sought,
Till in his soul affliction's rod
A peaceful moral wrought;

Till humbled at his Saviour's feet
  In penitence he lay,
And felt his pagan passions fleet
  On prayer's soft breath away.

Stern sickness rack'd his aged frame,
  Unwonted torpor stole,
And death all unresisted came
  To claim the ransom'd soul,
Which, spreading wide a wondering wing,
  With song of triumph past
From vengeful winter's sharpest sting,
  High o'er the shrieking blast.

Red torches pierced the midnight gloom
  As with the dead they hied,
And burst Beata's stony tomb
  To lay him by her side;
The lip so oft her sire that blest,
  No filial welcome gave,
As brow to brow, and breast to breast,
  They fill'd that frost-bound grave.

Strange music mid the funeral rite!
  Sad dirges, soft and slow!
Whence cometh, in this realm of night,
  Such melody of wo?
A chapel-bell! Who bids it speak
  In this forsaken bourne?
And thus, with Sabbath sweetness, break
  The trance of those who mourn?

Thou know'st not? Praise to God above!
The meek Moravian band,
With all their habitudes of love,
Have dared this fearful land:
Hast thou not heard how Greenland's wild,
Her everlasting snows,
Beneath their husbandry have smiled,
And blossom'd as the rose?

Their steps these saintly teachers turn'd
To yon sepulchral bed,
And o'er their buried convert mourn'd
As for a brother dead;
And there, with anthems' holy breath,
With prayers of heavenward trust,
They mark'd, as with a living wreath,
Poor Agusina's dust.

EARTH'S DELUSIONS.

Build'st thou on Wealth? Its wings are ever spread
 Its dazzled votaries to elude and foil!
On Science? Lo! the lofty sage hath fled,
 Like the pale lamp that lit his midnight toil,
 Forgotten as the flower that deck'd the vernal soil.

Build'st thou on Love? The trusting heart it cheers
 While youth and hope entwine their garlands gay,
Yet hath it still an heritage of tears:
 Build'st thou on Fame? The dancing meteor's ray
 Glides not on swifter wing, to deeper night away.

Why, on such sands, thy spirit's temple rear?
 How shall its base the wrecking billows shun?
Go, seek th' Eternal Rock, with humble fear,
 And on the tablet of each setting sun,
 Grave with a diamond pen some deed of duty done.

Young, art thou? then the words of Wisdom weigh
 Mature! the gathering ills of life beware.
Aged? Oh, make His changeless arm thy stay,
 Who saves the weakest suppliant from despair,
 And bids the darken'd tomb a robe of glory wear.

DEATH OF A YOUNG MAN DEVOTED TO MISSIONS.

Thou wert a musing student o'er thy book
When first I saw thee. Yet the eagle's wing
Soar'd not more duly sunward, than thy mind
From cliff to cliff of knowledge urged its way,
Kindling and glorying at the proud pursuit.
A ripe, rare spirit wrought within thy form
Of boyish beauty.

Then thy glance grew deep,
Feeding on secret, solitary thought
With speechless joy. For thou didst hear that voice
From voiceless nature, in the wind that swept
Around thy student's chamber, in the stream
Freshening the foliage of yon college grove,
And in the whisper of the lone wild flower,
Which none but poets hear. Thy waking lyre,
Sweet son of song, won thee warm brotherhood
From many a loving heart.

Yet not the realm
Of ancient learning, throng'd with classic shapes,
Nor rose-wreath'd poesy's enchanting bowers,
Contented thee.

Thy soul had higher aims,
And from Castalian waters meekly turn'd
To the pure rill that kiss'd the Saviour's feet:
And ever o'er its hour of lonely thought

Or deep devotion, China's millions stole,
Blind—wandering—lost.
So, then, thou didst dismiss
The host of pleasant fancies, which so long
Had made thy pilgrimage a music strain,
And for the outcast heathen pledge thy life,
A diamond to the treasury of thy Lord.
Heaven took the pledge, yet not for weary years
Of toil, and pain, and age.
There was a flush
On thy young cheek, a fire within thine eye,
A failing of the footstep, that was wont
To tread green earth so light and buoyantly,
A wasting of the half ethereal clay :
Heaven took the pledge, and thou art all its own.

APPROACH OF SPRING.

"For, lo, the winter is past."—*Solomon.*

God of each changing season,
  Creation speaks thy praise,
But souls endued with reason
  The highest strain should raise.

Lo! wintry tempests sweeping,
  No more deform the sky,
The crystal streamlet leaping
  Proclaimeth Spring is nigh.

Farewell the dark dominion
  Of tyrant frost and snow,
The robin spreads his pinion,
  And fragrant blossoms blow.

Awake to budding glory,
  Ye trees so long oppress'd,
So naked, scarr'd, and hoary,
  By wrecking winds distress'd.

Break forth, ye tuneful bowers,
  Where thousand warblers fly,
Unfold your robes, sweet flowers,
  The time of love is nigh.

Let the glad heart be pouring
  Such lays as angels sing,
Still to the bright world soaring
  Of everlasting Spring.

SCIENCE AND RELIGION.

"WHAT gives the mind this globe of earth to scan,
And chains brute instinct at the feet of man?
Bids the red comet on its car of flame
Reveal its periods and declare its name?
With deathless radiance gilds the historic page,
And reaps the laurels of a buried age?"
Majestic Science, from his cloister'd shrine,
Heard and replied, "This glorious power is mine."
"But say, canst thou the erring spirit lead,
That feels its weakness and deplores its need?
Canst thou the prison of despair illume?
Find sin a pardon, or disarm the tomb?"
With silent scorn the suppliant voice he spurn'd,
And to his ponderous tomes indignant turn'd.
Then from the cell, where long she dwelt apart,
Her humble mansion in the contrite heart,
Religion came; and where proud Science fail'd,
She bent her knee to earth, and with her Sire prevail'd.

THE DIVIDED BURDEN.

I SAW a boy who towards his cottage home
A heavy burden bore. The way was steep
And rocky, and his little loaded arm
Strain'd downward to its full extent, while wide
The other horizontally was thrown,
As if to counterpoise the painful weight
That drew him towards the earth.
A while he paused
And set his burden down, just where the path
Grew more precipitous, and wiped his brow
With his worn sleeve, and, panting, breathed long draughts
Of the sweet air, while the hot summer sun
Flamed o'er his forehead.
But another boy,
'Neath a cool poplar in a neighbouring field,
Sat playing with his dog, and from the grass
Uprising, with light bound the coppice clear'd,
And lent a vigorous hand to share the toil.
So on they went together, grasping firm
The basket's handle with a right good will;
And while their young, clear voices met my ear,
I recollected how the Bible said,
"Bear one another's burdens," and perceived
That to obey God's word was happiness.

Then, as the bee gleans from the humblest flower
Sown by the wayside honey for her hive,
I treasured up the lesson, and when eve
Call'd home the labouring ox, and to its bed
Warn'd the young bird, and shut the lily's cup,
I took my little boy upon my knee,
And told him of the basket-bearer's toil,
And of the friend who help'd him.
When his eye
Swell'd full and round, and fix'd upon my face,
Taking the story to his inmost soul,
I said, "My son, be pitiful to all,
And aid them when thou canst.
For God hath sown
Sweet seeds within us, seeds of sympathy,
Whose buds are virtues, such as bloom for heaven.

If thy young sister weepeth, kiss the tear
From her smooth cheek, and sooth with tender words
Her swelling breast; or if a secret thorn
Is in thy brother's bosom, draw it thence;
Or if thy playmate sorroweth, lend an ear,
And share with sympathy his weight of wo.

And when thou art a man, my little one,
Still keep thy spirit open to the ills
Of foreigner and stranger, of the race
Whom Afric's sun hath darken'd, and of those
Poor red-brow'd exiles from our forest shades,
Where once they ruled supreme.
Thus shalt thou shun
That selfishness which, wrapp'd in its own gifts,

Forgets alike the Giver and the grief
Of those who mourn.
So mayst thou ever find
Pity and love in thine own time of need,
If on thy young heart, as a signet ring,
Thou grav'st that motto from a Book Divine,
'Bear one another's burdens, and fulfil
The law of Christ.' "

THE SHIPWRECK.

The good ship on the iceberg struck, where northern seas were high,
And midnight wrapp'd in ebon veil the chill and starless sky:
It struck! what moment was there then to waste in sorrow's strife!
When but one bold adventurous rush remain'd 'tween death and life.

The boat! the boat! it launches forth upon the mountain wave,
And leaping throngs, with frantic haste, essay its power to save:
A fragile thing, it tossing strove amid the wrathful tide,
And deep, unutter'd pangs were theirs who left that vessel's side.

A moonbeam pierced the heavy cloud: oh, God! what sight was there!
Who stood upon that fated deck, in calm and mute despair!
A gentle maiden just aroused from slumber soft and dear,
Stretch'd her white arms in wild amaze, but found no helper near.

In fond adieu her hand she waved, as if some friend she bless'd,
Then closer drew her snowy robe around her youthful breast;

And upward to the darken'd heavens imploring glances cast,
While her rich curls profusely fell, and floated on the blast.

All sudden, from his wildering trance, a manly form did start,
While a loud agonizing cry burst from his labouring heart;
His bloodless lip was deadly cold, strange lustre fill'd his eye,
"How can I bear a brother's name, yet leave thee thus to die!"

He plunged—the crested wave he ruled; he climbed the cloven deck,
And clasp'd her as the thundering surge swept o'er the heaving wreck:
"Sweet sister, 'tis thy brother's voice; his cheek is pressed to thine;
Together childhood's path we trod, thy last dread couch be mine!"

Still look'd the moon with pitying eye, all lone and silent down,
Encircling them with holy light as with a martyr's crown,
Then shrank behind her fleecy veil; hoarse shrieked th' impetuous main;
The deep sea closed—and where were they? Ask of the angel train!

Ah! noble hearts that night were whelm'd beneath the billows high,
And temples white with honour'd years, and woman's love-lit eye,
And clinging to its mother's breast, in visions soft and deep,
Unwaken'd innocence went down amid the pearls to sleep.

The slumberers—they who sank that hour, without a struggling breath,
With whom the unbroken dream of life so melted into death,
Say, turn'd they not, in deep amaze, to seek the scenes of time,
When first eternity's dread shore spread out in pomp sublime?

Wo, wo was with the living heart! In many a smitten home,
Where, in the garniture of grief, the weeping inmates come,
Round many a lonely hearth-stone shall Memory's touch restore
The image of the loved and lost, who must return no more.

The eye that saw that monster-mass come drifting darkly down,
Destruction in its wintry blast and on its vitreous crown,
The ear that heard the deadly crash, the thunder of the wave,
Can never lose the bitter trace but in the oblivious grave.

The rescued man, to listening groups, shall tell the fearful tale,
And mute affection clasp his hand, and childhood's cheek be pale,
And while, with quicken'd heart, they bless the great Deliverer's care,
The iceberg and the buried ship shall prompt their tearful prayer.

X

PRAYER AT SEA.

PRAYER may be sweet in cottage homes,
Where sire and child devoutly kneel,
And through the open casement nigh
The vernal blossoms gently steal.

Prayer may be sweet in stately halls,
Where heart with kindred heart is blent,
And upward to the Eternal Throne
The hymn of praise melodious sent.

But he who fain would know how strong
The soul's appeal to God may be,
From friends and native land should turn,
A wanderer on the faithless sea:

Should hear its deep imploring tone
Rise upward o'er the thundering surge,
When breakers threat the fragile bark,
And winds with waves their conflict urge.

No spot on which his foot can rest,
No refuge where his form may flee,
How will he cling, oh Rock Divine,
And bind his anchoring hope to Thee.

GRASSMERE AND RYDAL WATER.

O VALE of Grassmere! tranquil, and shut out
From all the strife that shakes a jarring world,
How quietly thy village roofs are bower'd
In the cool verdure, while thy graceful spire
Guardeth the ashes of the noble dead,
And, like a fix'd and solemn sentinel,
Holm-Crag looks down on all.
And thy pure lake,
Spreading its waveless breast of crystal out
'Tween thee and us, pencil, nor lip of man
May fitly show its loveliness. The soul
Doth hoard it as a gem, and, fancy-led,
Explore its curving shores, its lonely isle,
That like an emerald clasp'd in crystal, sleeps.

Ho, stern Helvellyn! with thy savage cliffs
And dark ravines, where the rash traveller's feet
Too oft have wander'd far and ne'er return'd,
Why dost thou press so close yon margin green,
Like border-chieftain seeking for his bride
Some cottage-maiden? Prince amid the hills,
That each upon his feudal seat maintains
Strict sovereignty, hast thou a tale of love
For gentle Grassmere, that thou thus dost droop
Thy plumed helmet o'er her, and peruse
With such a searching gaze her mirror'd brow?

She listeneth coyly, and her guileless depths
Are troubled at a tender thought from thee.
And yet methinks some speech of love should dwell
In scenes so beautiful. For not in vain,
Nor with a feeble voice, doth He who spread
Such glorious charms bespeak man's kindliness
For all whom He hath made, bidding the heart
Grasp every creature, with a warm embrace
Of brotherhood.

Lo! what fantastic forms,
In sudden change, are traced upon the sky.
The sun doth subdivide himself, and shine
On either side of an elongate cloud,
Which, like an alligator huge and thin,
Pierceth his disk. And then an ostrich seem'd
Strangely to perch upon a wreath of foam,
And gaze disdainful on the kingly orb,
That lay o'erspent and weary. But he roused
Up as a giant, and the welkin glow'd
With rushing splendour, while his puny foes
Vanish'd in air. Old England's oaks outstretch'd
Their mighty arms, and took that cloudless glance
Into their bosoms, as a precious thing
To be remember'd long.

And so we turn'd,
And through romantic glades pursued our way,
Where Rydal Water spends its thundering force,
And through the dark gorge makes a double plunge
Abruptly beautiful. Thicket, and rock,
And ancient summer-house, and sheeted foam
All exquisitely blent, while deafening sound
Of torrents battling with their ruffian foes

Fill'd the admiring gaze with awe, and wrought
A dim forgetfulness of all beside.
 Thee, too, I found within thy sylvan home,
Whose music thrill'd my heart when life was new,
Wordsworth! with wild enchantment circled round,
In love with Nature's self, and she with thee.
Thy ready hand, that from the landscape cull'd
Its long familiar charms, rock, tree, and spire,
With kindness half paternal leading on
My stranger footsteps through the garden walk,
Mid shrubs and flowers that from thy planting grew;
The group of dear ones gathering round thy board—
She, the first friend, still as in youth beloved—
The daughter, sweet companion—sons mature,
And favourite grandchild, with his treasured phrase—
The evening lamp, that o'er thy silver locks
And ample brow fell fitfully, and touch'd
Thy lifted eye with earnestness of thought,
Are with me as a picture, ne'er to fade
Till death shall darken all material things.

THOUGHTS AT THE GRAVE OF SIR WALTER SCOTT.

Rest with the noble dead
  In Dryburgh's solemn pile,
Where sleep the peer and warrior bold,
And mitred abbots stern and old,
  Along the statued isle;
Where, stain'd with dust of buried years,
The rude sarcophagus appears
  In mould imbedded deep;
And Scotia's skies of sparkling blue
Stream the oriel windows through,
  Where ivied masses creep;
And, touch'd with symmetry sublime,
The moss-clad towers that mock at time
  Their mouldering legends keep.

And yet methinks thou shouldst have chose
  Thy latest couch at fair Melrose,
Whence burst thy first, most ardent song,
And swept with wildering force along
  Where Tweed in silver flows.
There the young moonbeams, quivering faint
O'er mural tablet sculptured quaint,
  Reveal a lordly race;
And knots of roses richly wrought,
And tracery light as poet's thought,
  The cluster'd columns grace.

There good King David's rugged mien
Fast by his faithful spouse is seen,
  And 'neath the stony floor
Lie chiefs of Douglas' haughty breast,
Contented now to take their rest,
  And rule their kings no more.

It was a painful thing to see
  Trim Abbotsford so gay,
The rose-trees climbing there so bold,
The ripening fruits in rind of gold,
  And thou, their lord, away.

I saw the lamp, with oil unspent,
O'er which thy thoughtful brow was bent,
  When erst, with magic skill,
Unearthly beings heard thy call,
And flitting spectres throng'd the hall,
  Obedient to thy will.

Yon fair domain was all thine own,
From stately roof to threshold stone,
  Yet didst thou lavish pay
The coin that caused life's wheels to stop?
The heart's blood oozing drop by drop
  Through the tired brain away?

I said the lamp unspent was there,
The books arranged in order fair;
But none of all thy kindred race
Found in those lordly halls a place:
Thine only son, in foreign lands,
Led boldly on his martial bands,

And stranger-lips, unmoved and cold,
The legends of thy mansion told;
They lauded glittering brand and spear,
And costly gifts of prince and peer,
And broad claymore, with silver dight,
And hunting-horn of border knight—
What were such gauds to me?
More dear had been one single word
From those whose veins thy blood had stirr'd
To Scotia's accents free.

Yet one there was, in humble cell,
A poor retainer, lone and old,
Who of thy youth remember'd well,
And many a treasured story told;
And pride, upon her wrinkled face,
Blent strangely with the trickling tear,
As Memory, from its choicest place,
Brought forth, in deep recorded trace,
Thy boyhood's gambols dear,
Or pointed out, with wither'd hand,
Where erst thy garden-seat did stand,
When thou return'd from travel vain,
Wrapp'd in thy plaid, and pale with pain,
Didst gaze with vacant eye,
For stern disease had drank the fount
Of mental vision dry.

Ah! what avails, with giant power,
To wrest the trophies of an hour;
One moment write, with sparkling eye,
Our name on castled turrets high,

And yield the next, a broken trust,
To earth, to ashes, and to dust.

And now farewell, whose hand did sweep
Away the damps of ages deep,
And fire with proud baronial strain
The harp of chivalry again,
And make its wild, forgotten thrill
To modern ears delightful still.

Thou, who didst make, from shore to shore,
Bleak Caledonia's mountains hoar,
Her blue lakes bosom'd in their shade,
Her sheepfolds scatter'd o'er the glade,
Her rills, with music, leaping down,
The perfume of her heather brown,
Familiar as their native glen
To differing tribes of distant men,
Patriot and bard! old Scotia's care
Shall keep thine image fresh and fair,
Embalming to remotest time
The Shakspeare of her tuneful clime.

FAREWELL TO EDINBURGH.

THE shade is on thy brow, sweet land,
The shade is on thy brow,
For autumn rends away the crown
That summer gave but now;
I turn me towards a greener clime,
Where Albion's groves appear,
But still the tear is on my cheek
For thee, Edina dear.

There may, perchance, be richer realms,
Where pride and splendour roll,
But thou hast, sure, the wealth of heart,
That wins the stranger's soul;
There may, perchance, be those who say
That Scotia's hills are drear,
Yet tears are lingering on my cheek
For thee, Edina dear.

And when, my pilgrim-wanderings o'er,
I seek my native-land,
And by my ingle-side once more
Do clasp the kindred hand,
And tell my listening children tales
Of climes of foreign fame,
Their grateful tears with mine will fall
At dear Edina's name.

STATUE OF THE SPINNING GIRL,

AT CHATSWORTH, THE SEAT OF THE DUKE OF DEVONSHIRE.

SPIN on, most beautiful.
There's none to mock
Thy simple labour here. Majestic forms
Of high renown, and brows of classic grace,
Whose sculptured features speak the breathing soul,
Rise in illustrious ranks, but not to scorn
Thy lowly toil.
Even so it was of old,
That woman's hand, amid the elements
Of patient industry and household good,
Reproachless wrought, twining the slender thread
From the light distaff, or in skilful loom
Weaving rich tissues, or with glowing tints
Of rich embroidery, pleased to decorate
The mantle of her lord. And it was well;
For in such shelter'd and congenial sphere
Content with duty dwelt.
Yet few there are,
Sweet Filatrice, who in their earnest task
Find such retreat as thine, mid lordly halls,
And sparkling fountains, and umbrageous trees,
And parks far stretching, where the antler'd deer
Forget the hound and horn.
And we, who roam
Mid all this grand enchantment—proud saloons,

And galleries radiant with the gems of art
And genius, ravish'd from the grasp of time—
And princely chapel, uttering praise to God—
Or lose ourselves amid the wildering maze
Of plants, and flowers, and blossoms, breathing forth
Their eloquence to Him—delighted lay
This slight memorial at thy snowy feet.

SHEEP ON THE CHEVIOT HILLS.

Graze on, graze on, there comes no sound
  Of border-warfare here,
No slogan cry of gathering clan,
  No battle-axe or spear;
No belted knight in armour bright,
  With glance of kindling ire,
Doth change the sports of Chevy-Chase
  To conflict stern and dire.

Ye wist not that ye press the spot
  Where Percy held his way
Across the marches, in his pride
  The "chiefest hearts to slay,"
And where the stout Earl Douglas rode
  Upon his milk-white steed,
With fifteen hundred Scottish spears
  To stay the invader's deed.

Graze on, graze on, there's many a rill,
  Wild wandering through the glade,
Where you may freely slake your thirst,
  With none to make afraid;
There's many a murmuring stream that flows
  From Cheviot's terraced side,
Yet not one drop of warrior's gore
  Distains its crystal tide.

For Scotia from her hills hath come,
  And Albion o'er the Tweed,
To give the mountain breeze the feuds
  That made their noblest bleed,
And like two friends, around whose hearts
  Some dire estrangement run,
Love all the closer for the past,
  And sit them down as one.

SEPARATION.

You've watch'd the lessening sail
  That bore the friend away,
Till but a misty speck it seem'd
  Upon the billowy bay;
The grating wheels you've mark'd
  In their receding flight,
Like victors vaunting, as they took
  Your treasure from your sight.

A sever'd tress you've hid
  Next to your bosom's core,
A plant, the parting token, nursed
  Till all its bloom was o'er;
Amid your choicest page
  Some wither'd flow'ret prest,
That erst a prouder place maintain'd
  Upon the dear one's breast.

You o'er the pencill'd brow
  In solitude have hung,
And to the voiceless picture talk'd
  With love's impassion'd tongue;
You've sought the favourite walk,
  Green dell, or sea-girt shore,
And felt how deep the shade had fallen
  On all that charm'd before:

Or to your secret bower
  In lonely sadness stole,
To muse o'er hoarded word and smile,
  Those jewels of the soul;
You've borne a precious name
  Upon your soul-breathed prayer,
And at the threshold of the skies
  Reposed your anxious care.

The unutter'd pang you've felt,
  The bursting tear represt,
And shut the rankling anguish close
  Within your burden'd breast;
Or worn the outward smile,
  The hollow greeting said,
Till darkly on the springs of life
  The smother'd sorrow fed.

To twine the spring-tide wreath,
  And mourn o'er autumn's bier,
The hope to win, the joy to lose,
  This is our history here;
To find the rose, whose bloom
  Nor thorn nor blight hath riven,
To meet, and never more to part,
  Is not of earth, but heaven.

THE DESOLATE COTTAGE.

There stands a cottage on the Owlbar Moor,
Just where its heathery blackness melts away
To England's mellower green. Fast by its side
Nestled the wheat-stack, firmly bound and shaped
Even like another roof-tree, witnessing
Fair harvest and good husbandry. Some sheep
Roam'd eastward o'er the common, nibbling close
The scanty blade, while towards the setting sun
A hillock stretch'd, o'ershadow'd by a growth
Of newly-planted trees. 'Twould seem the abode
Of rural plenty and content. Yet here
A desolate sorrow dwelt, such as doth wring
Plain honest hearts, when what had long been twined
With every fibre is dissected out.

Beneath the shelter of those lowly eaves
An only daughter made the parents glad
With her unfolding beauties. Day by day
She gather'd sweetness on her lonely stem,
The lily of the moorlands. They, with thoughts
Upon their humble tasks, how best to save
Their little gain, or make that little more,
Scarce knew that she was beautiful, yet felt
Strange thrall upon their spirits when she spoke
So musical, or from some storied page
Beguiled their evening hour.

And when the sire
Descanted long, as farmers sometimes will,
About the promise of his crops, and how
The neighbours envied that his corn should be
Higher than theirs, and how the man that hoped
Surely to thrive must leave his bed betimes,
Or of her golden cheese the mother told,
She with a filial and serene regard
Would seem to listen, her young heart away
Mid other things. For in her lonely room
She had companions that they knew not of—
Books that reveal the sources of the soul,
Deep meditations, high imaginings—
And ofttimes, when the cottage lamp was out,
She sat communing with them, while the moon
Look'd through her narrow casement fitfully.
Hence grew her brow so spiritual, and her cheek
Pale with the purity of thought, that gleam'd
Around her from above.
The buxom youth,
Nursed at the ploughshare, wondering eyed her charms,
Or of her aspen gracefulness of form
Spoke slightingly. Yet when they saw the fields
Her father till'd, well clad with ripening grain,
And knew he had no other heir beside,
They with unwonted wealth of Sunday clothes,
And huge red nosegays flaunting in their hands,
Were fain to woo her. And they marvell'd much
How the sweet fairy, with such quiet air
Of mild indifference, and with truthful words
Kind, yet determinate, withdrew herself
To chosen solitude, intent to keep
A maiden's freedom.

But in lonely walks,
What time the early violets richly blent
Their trembling colours with the vernal green,
A student boy, who dwelt among the hills,
Taught her of love. There rose an ancient tree,
The glory of their rustic garden's bound,
Around whose rough circumference of trunk
A garden seat was wreathed; and there they sat,
Watching gray-vested twilight, as she bore
Such gifts of tender and half-utter'd thought
As lovers prize. When the thin-blossom'd furze
Gave out its autumn-sweetness, and the walls
Of that low cot with the red-berried ash
Kindled in pride, they parted; he to toil
Amid his college tasks, and she to weep.
—The precious scrolls, that with his ardent heart
So faithfully were tinged, unceasing sought
Her hand, and o'er their varied lines to pore
Amid his absence, was her chief delight.

—At length they came not. She with sleepless eye,
And lip that every morn more bloodless grew,
Demanded them in vain. And then the tongue
Of a hoarse gossip told her he was *dead—*
Drowned in the deep, and dead.

Her young heart died
Away at these dread sounds. Her upraised eye
Grew large and wild, and never closed again.
"Hark! Hark! He calleth! I must hence away!"
She murmur'd oft, but faint and fainter still.
Nor other word she spake. And so she died.

—And now that cottage on the Owlbar Moor
Hath no sweet visitant of earthly hope
To cheer its toiling inmates. Habit-led,
They sow and reap, and spread the humble board,
But steep their bread in tears.
God grant them grace
To take his chastisement, like those who gain
A more enduring substance from the blast
That leaveth house and heart so desolate.

THE ELM-TREES.

I do remember me
  Of two old elm-trees' shade,
With mosses sprinkled at their feet,
  Where my young childhood play'd ;
While the rocks above their head
  Frown'd out so stern and gray,
And the little crystal streamlet near
  Went leaping on its way.

There, side by side, they flourish'd,
  With intertwining crown,
And through their broad embracing arms
  The prying moon look'd down ;
And I deem'd, as there I linger'd—
  A musing child, alone—
She sought my secret heart to scan
  From her far silver throne.

I do remember me
  Of all their wealth of leaves,
When summer, in her radiant loom,
  The burning solstice weaves ;
And how, with firm endurance,
  They braved an adverse sky,
Like Belisarius, doom'd to meet
  His country's wintry eye.

I've roam'd through varied regions,
  Where stranger-streamlets run,
And where the proud magnolia flaunts
  Beneath a southern sun,
And where the sparse and stinted pine
  Puts forth its sombre form,
A vassal to the arctic cloud,
  And to the tyrant storm,

And where the pure unruffled lakes
  In placid wavelets roll,
Or where sublime Niagara shakes
  The wonder-stricken soul,
I've seen the temple's sculptured pile,
  The pencil's glorious art,
Yet still those old green trees I wore
  Depictured on my heart.

Years fled; my native vale I sought,
  Where those tall elm-trees wave;
But many a column of its trust
  Lay broken in the grave.
The ancient and the white-hair'd men,
  Whose wisdom was its stay,
For them I ask'd, and Echo's voice
  Made answer, "*Where are they?*"

I sought the thrifty matron,
  Whose busy wheel was heard
When the early beams of morning
  Awoke the chirping bird;

Strange faces from her window look'd,
  Strange voices fill'd her cot,
And, 'neath the very vine she train'd,
  Her memory was forgot.

I left a youthful mother,
  Her children round her knee,
Those babes had risen into men,
  And coldly look'd on me;
But she, with all her bloom and grace,
  Did in the churchyard lie,
While still those changeless elms upbore
  Their kingly canopy.

Though we, who 'neath their lofty screen
  Pursued our childish play,
May show amid our sunny locks
  Some lurking tints of gray,
And though the village of our love
  Doth many a change betide,
Still do those sacred elm-trees stand,
  In all their strength and pride.

THE YOUNG MOTHER.

THERE sat upon the parent's knee,
In love supremely bless'd,
An infant, fair and full of glee,
Caressing and caress'd,
While siren Hope, with gladness wild,
And eye cerulean blue,
Bent sweetly down to kiss the child,
And bless the mother too.

Then Memory came, with serious mien,
And, looking back the while,
Cast such a shadow o'er the scene
As dimm'd Affection's smile;
For still to Fancy's brightest hours
She gave a hue of care,
And bitter odours tinged the flowers
That wreathed her sunny hair.

But in the youthful mother's soul
Each cloud of gloom was brief,
Too pure her raptured feelings roll
To take the tint of grief;
Firm Faith around her idol boy
Its radiant mantle threw,
And claim'd for him a higher joy
Than Hope or Memory knew.

THE MILLINERS AND FISHES.

COMMERCE and enterprise should be applauded,
And so the Paris milliners opine
It seems ; for when their fashionable fabrics
Grow obsolete, 'tis said they freight a vessel
Straight for the Baltic, and the Northern belles
In the quaint fragments of the realm of taste,
Proudly array themselves. And yet 'twere sad,
Methinks, to see, at polar fête or ball,
Some shivering Nova-Zemblan lady flaunt
In robe of lace, short-sleeved, the purple bust
Reveal'd most liberally.

Once a storm,
Hoarse from the Gulf of Finland, crossly wreck'd
The adventurous ship quite near her destined port,
And strew'd her riches o'er the admiring deep.
There perish'd many a hope of many a fair
Young sempstress, by such cruel loss condemn'd
To wear her cast-off dress another year,
Vamp'd up as best she may.

'Tis an ill wind
That blows no good. The watery realm rejoiced,
For all its finny aristocracy
Of their oldfashioned suits had long complain'd.
Next day a Salmon at the Neva's mouth
Was taken, very delicately clad
In a white lutestring drapery, with veil

Z

Of costly blonde: her wedding dress, no doubt.
The bridemaid, Porpoise, wore a radiant zone
Girt rather tight around the slender waist,
While her embroider'd mouchoir snugly hid
A bottle of Cologne to cheer the bride
During the service. Ogling, near the shore
A Sturgeon stole, her finery to display:
A very stiff brocade, with bishop sleeves,
Making such huge circumference 'twere well
She had no neighbour near; while a smart hat
Envelop'd in its rich rotundity
Her fairy brow.
The Seal was taking snuff,
And thrust his box in a bead reticule;
The other rough paw held a parasol
Of parti-colour'd silk, and ivory-staff'd:
'Twas thought the Amphibia, one and all, would find
This fashion quite commodious, in their walks
To leave their cards beneath the summer sun.

—A Shark in a small boat's wake follow'd long;
The sailors thought his purpose was to eat them,
And spread all sail; *but 'twas to be unlaced,*
For he a pair of corsets had rigg'd on,
With busk and bones, just fashionably tight,
But could not bear the torture; so with haste
Panting and flouncing, sought to be released.
Item: Would it not be the surest way
To kill that hardy and voracious fish,
Which ofttimes foils the harpoon?
Mighty mounds
Of artificial flowers did make the deep

Glow like a greenhouse. Full frisets and curls
Lay unregarded, till a prudish Pike,
Suspected to be somewhat in her wane,
Assumed a wig, declaring it more cool,
And vastly more delightful to the head
Than was the natural hair.
Such varied stores
Of gay gauze robes on seaweed hedges hung,
That the plebeians thought to have a ball
In the old Coral Palace. Thither came
The Codlings, deck'd with drooping Ostrich-plumes,
The purblind Lampreys, each with opera-glass
Uplifted pertly, and gay safety-chain
The gilded watch within their belts to guard;
The Lobsters toiling their red arms to hide
'Neath long kid gloves, and their strange nether limbs
Ensconced in gaiter-boots; while countless shoals
Of Herrings flock'd, false brilliants in their heads
In gorgeous knots; and Crabs with widespread fans,
Aping the elegant, but inly chafed
To find their retrograding step confound
Their partners, figuring in the favourite waltz.

—A barge of Oysters reach'd St. Petersburgh:
Extremely loth they were to be dissected,
For those sly people in their cloister'd cells,
Close-mouth'd as Achan with his wedge of gold,
Lock'd hoards of jewelry, broaches and rings
Profuse as ancient Cannæ's battle spoil.

—Even thus it is. What bodeth loss to one
Doth prove another's gain. The adversity

Of those French milliners did benefit
The commonwealth of fishes. A few tears,
Brief and soon dried, fill'd the broad sea with joy
And merry pastime. One small spot of earth
Was sad, but what a gorgeous holyday
Held Ocean's myriads!
Sure the tuneful bard
Of Twickenham hath not unjustly styled
"*All partial evil universal good.*"

THE KING OF THE ICEBERGS.

SERENE the Sabbath evening fell
  Upon the Northern deep,
And lonely there a noble bark
  Across the waves did sweep;
She rode them like a living thing,
  That heeds not blast nor storm,
When, lo! the King of the Icebergs rose,
  A strange and awful form.

Upon the horizon's verge he frown'd,
  A mountain mid the main,
As erst Philistia's giant tower'd
  O'er Israel's tented plain.
And hoarsely o'er the dark blue sea
  Was a threat'ning challenge toss'd,
"Who is this, that dares, with feet of fire,
  To tread in my realm of frost?"

Yet on the gallant steamship went,
  Her heart of flame beat high,
And the stream of her fervent breath flow'd out
  In volumes o'er the sky!
So the Ice-King seized his deadly lance
  To pierce the stranger foe,
And down to his deed of vengeance rush'd,
  Troubling the depths below.

The watchful stars look'd calmly on,
  Girt with their silver zones,
When a flash of bursting glory traced
  An arch around their thrones.
For Aurora Borealis bent
  From her palace above the skies,
And the wondering billows open'd wide
  Their phosphorescent eyes.

Firm at his post the captain stood,
  Clear-soul'd and undismay'd,
And the King of the Iceberg's power defied,
  While night drew on its shade;
On, through the interdicted realm,
  With fearless prow he sped,
Though round him gathering dangers press'd,
  And nameless forms of dread.

And longer had he borne the strife,
  But he thought of those who gave
Their life and welfare to his hand
  Upon the faithless wave;
The noble and the true of heart,
  The helpless and the fair,
The child upon its mother's knee,
  That knew no fear nor care;

And felt, in their far-distant homes,
  How deep the grief and sore,
If the lip of love for them should ask,
  And they return no more.

And so his gallant ship he steer'd
  From the disastrous fray,
And full in the teeth of the southern blast
  Led on her venturous way.

"Not thus shall ye 'scape my stormy ire,"
  The King of the Icebergs spake,
And bade unloose his vassal train,
  By arctic stream and lake;
And swift a countless monster train
  Rode over the waters blue,
With their dazzling helms and stony eyes,
  A pitiless, ruffian crew.

An icy ambush around the keel
  With breathless speed they laid,
And the vengeful monarch laugh'd to see
  How strong that mesh was made;
And, clustering close, that squadron dire
  Spread over the startled flood,
While their arrows of frost flew thick, and chill'd
  The hardiest seaman's blood.

But there fell a gleam of the light above,
  That with Mercy's angel dwells,
And aided the labouring bark to foil
  The King of the Iceberg's spells:
For this, by many a hearth-stone bright,
  A strain of praise shall be,
To him who guides the wanderer home,
  And rules the boisterous sea.

VALE OF THE MOHAWK.

Vale of the Mohawk, freshly green,
What beauty in thy bound is seen!
What verdure clothes thy fair retreats,
How revels every gale in sweets!
Each leaf with dewy lustre shining,
Each vine with strong embrace entwining,
And where thy rich alluvial glows,
And full-gorged Plenty seeks repose,
It seems that scarce the hand of toil
Need vex the bosom of the soil,
So kindly Earth the seed receives,
So free returns the weight of sheaves.
And there thy river, pure and sheen,
Flows on, its fringed banks between,
Proud of its realm, and pleased to glide
To meet old Hudson's mightier tide.
From meads of clover rich and high
We saw the plundering bees go by,
And yet they scarce the surface stirr'd
Of sweets, on which the expecting herd
Shall banquet, when the mowers blithe
In the shorn flower-cups dip their scythe.
We saw the reaper girded meet
To sweep away the ripen'd wheat:
But to his throat advancing high
Its bearded lance and russet eye,

He stoutly wrestled on his way,
Like swimmer with the billowy bay,
Till all behind his path of toil
Lay in dead waves, the harvest-spoil.

—While we, of bleak New-England's coast,
That ne'er a mine of wealth might boast,
Save what her sons laborious find
Who dig the quarry of the mind,
(And, certes, they such wealth who hold,
May well contemn the lust of gold)
We, still delighted and amazed,
Upon these haunts of richness gazed,
Nor spared to praise, with heart elate,
The splendour of the "Empire State:"
—But lauded more, in accents bland,
The glory of our Native Land,
Who, if she simply understood
The flowing fulness of her good,
And felt her blessings as she ought,
And praised her Maker in her thought,
And did His will, might surely be
The very happiest of the free.

LOVE OF WEALTH.

O Earth! thou gorged and mighty sepulchre!
How find'st thou room for all the born of clay,
From him, the sire of Eden, to the babe
That gasps this hour?
Why need we join the race
For shadows on thy surface? hastening on
Ourselves like shadows, to the common home
That waits the dead.
What boots a broad domain,
A lordly heritage, for which are feuds,
Heart-burnings, and, perchance, a brother's blood?

—Show me the face, upon thy country's map,
Of that estate which lust hath coveted
And fraud obtain'd. Show me its waving trees,
Its pleasant hillocks, and its corn-clad vales.
Thou canst not! Boast they not one narrow space
Upon the picture? Yet for this a soul
Hath lost its place in Heaven!
And shall we throw
Love, truth, and conscience in the ill-poised scale,
Bidding some little modicum of gold
Outweigh them all?
I thought that I had read
There was a judgment, where the deeds of men
Met just reward. But they who lightly look

Upon the shifting face of things, might deem
God's page of truth reversed, and that the gain
Of wealth was what the denizens of earth
Did chiefly toil and strive for, and the words
" *Get rich*" had been sole passport to heaven's gate.

MUTATIONS.

As waves the grass upon the fields to-day,
Which soon the wasting scythe shall sweep away,
As smiles the flow'ret in the morning dew,
Which eve's chill blast in blighted death may strew,
Thus in brief glory spring the sons of clay,
Thus bloom a while, then wither and decay.

I saw an infant in its robe of white,
The admiring mother's ever dear delight;
It clapp'd its hands when tones of mirth went by,
And nature's gladness glisten'd in its eye;
Again I came—an empty crib was there,
A little coffin, and a funeral prayer.

I saw a boy in healthful vigour bold,
Nor summer's heat he fear'd, nor winter's cold,
With dexterous foot he dared the frozen pool,
His laugh rang loudest mid his mates at school;
Again I came—his name alone was found
On one low stone that marks yon churchyard mound.

I saw a gentle maid with beauty bless'd,
In youth resplendent, and by love caress'd,
Her clustering hair in sunny ringlets glow'd,
Her red lips moved, and thrilling music flow'd;
Again I came—her parents' halls were lone,
And o'er her turf-bed rose the weeper's moan.

Oh boasted joys of earth! how swift ye fly,
Rent from the heart or hidden from the eye;
So through the web the weaver's shuttle glides,
So speeds the vessel o'er the billowy tides,
So cleaves the bird the liquid fields of light,
And leaves no furrow of its trackless flight.

Dust tends to dust, with ashes, ashes blend,
Yet when the grave ingulfs the buried friend,
A few brief sighs may mark its yawning brink,
A few salt tears the broken clods may drink,
A few sad hearts with bursting anguish bleed,
And pay that tribute which they soon must need.

They soon must need! But life's returning cares
Sweep off the precious fruit that sorrow bears;
The mourner drops his sable, and aspires
To light anew ambition's smother'd fires,
Bathes his worn brow with labour's wasting dew,
And sleepless toils for heirs he knows not who.

Then He who marks us in our vain career,
Oft smites in mercy what we hold most dear,
Shreds from our vine the bowering leaves away,
And breaks its tendrils from their grovelling stay,
That the rich clusters, lifted to the sky,
May ripen better for a world on high.

RETURN OF THE PASTOR.

Thou who on the mighty deep
Didst our friend, our pastor keep,
On the billows' angry breast
Lull him like a babe to rest,
While beneath their watery floor
Thousands sank to rise no more,
Here, within this temple-shrine,
Father! let the praise be thine.

Thou who from a foreign sky,
Strangers' hearth and strangers' eye,
Bore him to his native strand,
To the green hills of our land,
To the home where love and prayer
Watch'd for him with ceaseless care,
Here, within this temple-shrine,
Father! let the praise be thine.

Sickness had an arrow dire
Dipp'd for him in fever's fire,
Spread an ambush dark with strife
Round the fountain-head of life,
Thou! who from the yawning grave
Raised him up to guide and save,
Here, within this temple-shrine,
Father! let the praise be thine.

OUR TEACHERS.

"I feel that the dead have conferred a blessing on me, by helping me to think of the world rightly."—*Rev. Orville Dewey.*

SAY'ST thou the dead are *teachers?*
Must we come,
And sit among the clods, and lay our ear
To the damp crannies of the loathsome tomb,
And listen for their lore?
There comes no sound
From all those stern and stone-bound sepulchres.
Grassblades are there, and flowers, and now and then
A mother-bird doth cheer her callow young
With chirping strain; while the low winds that sweep
The shivering harp-strings of yon ancient pines
Make sullen undulation.
Still thou say'st
The silent dead are teachers.
Stretch your hands,
And on our tablets write one pencil-trace,
That we may hoard it in our heart of hearts.
All motionless! All passionless! All mute!
O silence! twin with wisdom! I would press
My lip upon yon cradled infant's grave,
And drink the murmur of its smitten bloom.
A mother's young pride in her beautiful,
Her darling ministries from eve to morn,

Laid low! Laid low! How slight the aspen stem
Round which her heart's joys twined. Yet all are frail,
All like the crisp stalk in the reaper's path.

—Read I thy lesson right, my little one?
See, by thy side, the strong man sleepeth well.
The tall, proud man, who tower'd, like Israel's king,
With head above the people. Yet his wail,
Was it not weak as thine when death launch'd home
The fatal dart? Humility befits
The born of earth, the crush'd before the moth;
And the deep teaching of such lowly creed
Best cometh from the dead.
Ah! let me kneel
Here on this mound, where sleeps my early friend,
And wait her words in lowliness of soul.
Thou speak'st not to me! thou whose silver tone
Did lead the way, in all our sweet discourse,
When, lost in lonely haunts, we wander'd long,
Shunning the crowd. Twin-soul thou wert with mine.
Yet still I think I loved thee not enough
When thou wert with me.
Thy clear, welcome voice,
Thy soft caress at meeting, it would seem
That sometimes clouds around my spirit hung,
Checking the fond response. Beloved one,
Was it not so? And there were tender words
I might have said to thee, and said them not.
And there were higher flights of glorious thought,
And nobler trophies on life's rugged steep,
To which I might have urged thee. Was it so?
Make answer from thy pillow. Blind and weak!

I thought to have thee ever by my side.
And so the hours swept by, till thou didst spread
A sudden wing, and prove thine angel-birth.

O, by the keen regret of those lost hours,
Pure spirit! teach me with firm grasp to seize
The passing moment, not with duty's deed,
Or the defrauded sympathies of love,
To load the uncertain future; but with prayer
Propitiate Him who metes our fleeting days,
And teacheth wisdom from the voiceless tomb.

LIFE'S EVENING.

"Abide with us, for it is now evening, and the day of life is far spent."
BISHOP ANDREWS.

THE bright and blooming morn of youth
  Hath faded from the sky,
And the fresh garlands of our hope
  Are wither'd, sere, and dry;
O Thou, whose being hath no end,
  Whose years can ne'er decay,
Whose strength and wisdom are our trust,
  Abide with us, we pray.

Behold the noonday sun of life
  Doth seek its western bound,
And fast the lengthening shadows cast
  A heavier gloom around,
And all the glow-worm lamps are dead,
  That, kindling round our way,
Gave fickle promises of joy—
  Abide with us, we pray.

Dim eve draws on, and many a friend
  Our early path that bless'd,
Wrapp'd in the cerements of the tomb,
  Have laid them down to rest;
But Thou, the Everlasting Friend,
  Whose Spirit's glorious ray
Can gild the dreary vale of death,
  Abide with us, we pray.

THE WINTER NOSEGAY.

Flowers! fresh flowers, with your fragrance free,
Have you come in your queenly robes to *me?*
Me have you sought from your far retreat,
With your greeting lips and your dewy feet,
And the upward glance of your radiant eye,
Like angel-guests from a purer sky?

But where did ye hide when the frost drew near,
And your many sisters were blanched with fear?
Where did ye hide? with a blush as bright
As ye wore amid Eden's vales of light,
Ere the wile of the tempter its bliss had shamed,
Or the terrible sword o'er its gateway flamed.

Flowers, sweet flowers, with your words of cheer,
Thanks to the friend who hath sent you here;
For this, may her blossoms of varied dye
Be the fairest and first 'neath a vernal sky,
And she be led, by their whisper'd lore,
To the love of that land where they fade no more.

THE END.

VALUABLE WORKS

PUBLISHED BY

HARPER & BROTHERS, NEW-YORK.

HISTORY.

Manners and Customs of the Japanese, in the Nineteenth Century. From the Accounts of recent Dutch Residents in Japan, and from the German Work of DR. PH. FR. Von Siebold. 18mo.

Ruins of Ancient Cities; with general and particular Accounts of their Rise, Fall, and present Condition. By Charles Bucke. 2 vols. 18mo.—90 cents.

Mosheim's Institutes of Ecclesiastical History, Ancient and Modern, in four Books, much Corrected, Enlarged, and Improved, from the Primary Authorities. A new and literal Translation from the original Latin, with copious additional Notes, original and selected. By James Murdock, D.D. 3 vols. 8vo. Sheep extra.

Gibbon's History of the Decline and Fall of the Roman Empire. New Edition. With Notes, by M. Guizot and Rev. H. H. Milman. Complete in 4 vols. 8vo. With Maps and Engravings. Sheep extra.

The History of Modern Europe: with a View of the Progress of Society, from the rise of the modern Kingdoms to the Peace of Paris in 1763. By William Russell, LL.D.: and a Continuation of the History to the present Time, by William Jones, Esq. With Annotations by an American. In 3 vols. 8vo. With Engravings, &c. Sheep extra.

The Historical Works of William Robertson, D.D. 3 vols. 8vo. With Maps, Engravings, &c. Sheep extra. —$5 00.

The History of the Discovery and Settlement of America. By William Robertson, D.D. With an Account of his Life and Writings. To which are added, Questions for the Examination of Students. By John Frost, A.M. In one vol. 8vo With a Portrait and Engravings. Sheep extra.

The History of the Reign of the Emperor Charles V.; with a View of the Progress of Society in Europe, from the Subversion of the Roman Empire to the Beginning of the Sixteenth Century. By William Robertson, D.D. To which are added, Questions for the Examination of Students. By John Frost, A.M. In one vol. 8vo. With Engravings. Sheep extra

The History of Scotland, during the Reigns of Queen Mary and of King James VI., till his Accession to the Crown of England. With a Review of the Scottish History previous to that Period. Including the History of India. 8vo. Sheep extra.

View of the State of Europe during the Middle Ages. By Henry Hallam. From the sixth London Edition. Complete in one volume, 8vo. Sheep extra.—$2 00.

Introduction to the Literary History of Europe during the Fifteenth, Sixteenth, Seventeenth, and Eighteenth Centuries. By Henry Hallam. 2 vols. 8vo.—$3 75

Rollin's Ancient History of the Egyptians, Carthaginians, Assyrians, Babylonians, Medes and Persians, Grecians, and Macedonians; including the History of the Arts and Sciences of the Ancients. With a Life of the Author, by James Bell. First complete American Edition. 8vo. Embellished with nine Engravings, including three Maps. Sheep extra.—$3 50. Bound in 2 vols., $3 75.

Prideaux's Connexions; or, the Old and New Testaments connected, in the History of the Jews and neighbouring Nations, from the Declension of the Kingdoms of Israel and Judah to the Time of Christ. By Humphrey Prideaux, D.D. New Edition. In 2 vols. 8vo. With Maps and Engravings. Sheep extra.—$3 75.

The History of Christianity, from the

Birth of Christ to the Abolition of Paganism in the Roman Empire. By the Rev. H. H. Milman. [In Press.]

A History of the Church, from the earliest Ages to the Reformation. By the Rev. George Waddington, M.A. 8vo.—$1 75.

History of Scotland. By Sir Walter Scott, Bart. 2 vols. 12mo.—$1 20.

History of France. By E. E. Crowe, Esq. 3 vols. 12mo.—$1 75.

History of the Netherlands to the Revolution of 1830. By T. C. Grattan, Esq. 12mo.—60 cents.

History of England to the Seventeenth Century. By Sir James Mackintosh. 3 vols. 12mo.—$1 50.

History of Spain and Portugal. By S. A. Dunham, LL.D. 5 vols. 12mo.—$2 50.

History of Switzerland. Edited by the Rev. Dionysius Lardner, LL.D. In one volume 12mo.—60 cents.

History of the Italian Republics. By J. L. de Sismondi. 12mo.—60 cents.

An Historical and Descriptive Account of Iceland, Greenland, and the Faroe Islands. 18mo. Maps and Engravings.—45 cents.

The History of the United States. By the Hon. S Hale. 2 vols. 18mo. (An original work.

The History of England. From the earliest Period to 1839. By Thomas Keightley. With Notes, &c., by the American Editor. 5 vols. 18mo.—$2 25.

Universal History, from the Creation of the World to the Decease of George III., 1820. By the Hon. Alexander Fraser Tytler and Rev. E. Nares, D.D. Edited by an American. In 6 vols. 18mo.

The History of Greece. By Dr. Goldsmith. Prepared by the Author of "American Popular Lessons," &c. 18mo.

The History of Rome. By Dr. Goldsmith. Edited by H. W. Herbert, Esq. 18mo.

Athens: its Rise and Fall; with Views of the Literature, Philosophy, and Social Life of the Athenian People. By Sir E. Lytton Bulwer, M.P., M.A. 2 vols. 12mo.—$1 20.

A Narrative of Events connected with the Rise and Progress of the Protestant Episcopal Church in Virginia. To which is added an Appendix, containing the Journals of the Conventions in Virginia from the Commencement to the present Time. By F. L Hawks. 8vo.—$1 75.

Luther and the Lutheran Reformation. By the Rev. John Scott, A.M. 2 vols. 18mo. Portraits.—$1 00.

History of the Reformed Religion in France. By the Rev. E. Smedley. 3 vols. 18mo. Engravings.—$1 40.

The History of the Jews. From the earliest Period to the present Time. By the Rev. H. H. Milman. 3 vols. 18mo. Engravings, Maps, &c.—$1 20.

A View of Ancient and Modern Egypt. With an Outline of its Natural History. By the Rev. M. Russell, LL.D. 18mo. Engravings.

History of Poland. From the earliest Period to the present Time. By James Fletcher, Esq. 18mo. Portrait.

Sacred History of the World, as displayed in the Creation and subsequent Events to the Deluge. Attempted to be philosophically considered in a Series of Letters to a Son. By Sharon Turner, F.S.A. 3 vols. 18mo.—$1 35.

History of the Bible. By the Rev. G. R. Gleig. 2 vols. 18mo. Map.—80 cents.

History of Chivalry and the Crusades. By G. P. R. James. 18mo. Engravings.

Sketches from Venetian History. By the Rev. E. Smedley, M.A. 2 vols. 18mo. Engravings.

Historical and Descriptive Account of British India. From the most remote Period to the present Time. By Hugh Murray, Esq., James Wilson, Esq., R. K. Greville, LL.D., Whitelaw Ainslie, M.D., William Rhind, Esq., Professor Jameson, Professor Wallace, and Captain Clarence Dalrimple. 3 vols. 18mo. Engravings.—$1 35.

Palestine, or the Holy Land. From the earliest Period to the present Time. By the Rev. M. Russell, LL.D. 18mo. Engravings.

History of Ireland. From the Anglo-Norman Invasion till the Union o the Country with Great Britain. By W. C. Taylor, Esq. With Additions, by William Sampson, Esq. 2 vols. 18mo. Engravings.

HISTORY.

Historical View of the Progress of Discovery on the Northern Coasts of North America. From the earliest Period to the present Time. By P. F. Tytler, Esq. With descriptive Sketches of the Natural History of the North American Regions. By Professor Wilson. 18mo. With a Map, &c.

Nubia and Abyssinia. Comprehending the Civil History, Antiquities, Arts, Religion, Literature, and Natural History. By the Rev. M. Russell, LL.D. 18mo. Map and Engravings. —45 cents.

The History of Arabia, Ancient and Modern. Containing a Description of the Country—An Account of its Inhabitants, Antiquities, Political Condition, and early Commerce—The Life and Religion of Mohammed —The Conquests, Arts, and Literature of the Saracens—The Caliphs of Damascus, Bagdad, Africa, and Spain—The Government and Religious Ceremonies of the Modern Arabs, &c. By Andrew Crichton. 2 vols. 18mo. Engravings, &c. — 90 cents.

An Historical Account of the Circumnavigation of the Globe, and of the Progress of Discovery in the Pacific Ocean, from the Voyage of Magellan to the Death of Cook. 18mo. With numerous Engravings.

Historical and Descriptive Account of Persia. From the earliest period to the present Time. With a detailed View of its Resources, Government, Population, Natural History, and the Character of its Inhabitants, particularly of the Wandering Tribes; including a Description of Afghanistan. By James B. Fraser, Esq. 18mo. Map, &c.

History and Present Condition of the Barbary States. Comprehending a View of their Civil Institutions, Arts, Religion, Literature, Commerce, Agriculture, and Natural Productions. By the Rev. M. Russell, LL.D. 18mo. Engravings.

A Compendious History of Italy. Translated from the original Italian. By Nathaniel Greene. 18mo. — 45 cents.

The Chinese: a general Description of the Empire of China and its Inhabitants. By John Francis Davis, F.R.S. 2 vols. 18mo. With Illustrative Engravings.

Historical and Descriptive Account of British America; comprehending Canada, Upper and Lower, Nova Scotia, New-Brunswick, Newfoundland, Prince Edward Island, the Bermudas, and the Fur Countries, &c By Hugh Murray, F.R.S.E. 2 vols. 18mo.

Outline History of the Fine Arts: with Notices of the Character and Works of many celebrated Artists. By Benson J. Lossing. 18mo. With 60 Engravings.

History of the Moors of Spain. Translated from the French Original of M. Florian. 18mo.

Festivals, Games, and Amusements, Ancient and Modern. By Horatio Smith, Esq. With Additions, by Samuel Woodworth, Esq., of New-York. 18mo. Engravings.—45 cents.

History of Connecticut. By Theodore Dwight, Esq. 18mo.

Xenophon. (Anabasis, translated by Edward Spelman, Esq., Cyropædia, by the Hon. M. A. Cooper.) 2 vols. 18mo. Portrait.

Sallust. Translated by William Rose, M.A. With Improvements. 18mo. —40 cents.

Cæsar. Translated by William Duncan. 2 vols. 18mo. Portrait.—90 cents.

Thucydides. Translated by William Smith, A.M. 2 vols. 18mo. Portrait. —90 cents.

Livy. Translated by George Baker, A.M. 5 vols. 18mo. Portrait.

Herodotus. Translated by the Rev. William Beloe. 3 vols. 18mo. Portrait.

History of New-York. By William Dunlap. 2 vols. 18mo. Engravings. —90 cents.

The History of the American Theatre. By William Dunlap. 8vo.

Discourses and Addresses on Subjects of American History, Arts, and Literature. By Gulian C. Verplanck. 12mo.

History of Priestcraft in all Ages and Countries. By William Howitt. 12mo.

The Condition of Greece. By Col. J. P. Miller. 12mo.

Full Annals of the Revolution in France, 1830. To which is added a particular Account of the Celebration of said Revolution in the City of New-

York, on the 25th November, 1830. By Myer Moses. 12mo.

Tales from American History. By the Author of "American Popular Lessons." 3 vols. 18mo. Engravings. —$1 00.

Uncle Philip's Conversations with the Children about the History of Virginia. 18mo. Engravings.

Uncle Philip's Conversations with the Children about the History of New-York. 2 vols. 18mo. Engravings—70 cents.

Uncle Philip's Conversations with the Children about the History of Massachusetts. 2 vols. 18mo. Engravings. —70 cents.

Uncle Philip's Conversations with the Children about the History of New-Hampshire. 2 vols. 18mo. Engravings.

Tales of the American Revolution. By B. B. Thatcher, Esq. 18mo.—35 cents.

Lost Greenland; or, Uncle Philip's Conversations with the Children about the Lost Colonies of Greenland. 18mo. With Engravings.—35 cents

BIOGRAPHY.

The Martyrs of Science; or, the Lives of Galileo, Tycho Brahe, and Kepler. By Sir David Brewster, K.H. 18mo. —45 cents.

Life of Rev. John Summerfield. By Holland, Esq. With additional Selections from his Correspondence. Edited by Rev. Daniel Smith. 8vo.

LIBRARY OF AMERICAN BIOGRAPHY. Edited by Jared Sparks, Esq. 10 vols. 12mo. Portraits.—$7 50.

Vol. I. contains Life of John Stark, by E. Everett.—Life of Charles Brockden Brown, by W. H. Prescott.—Life of Richard Montgomery, by John Armstrong.—Life of Ethan Allen, by Jared Sparks.

Vol. II. Life of Alexander Wilson, by Wm. B. O. Peabody.—Life of Captain John Smith, by George S. Hilliard.

Vol. III. Life and Treason of Benedict Arnold, by Jared Sparks.

Vol. IV. Life of Anthony Wayne, by John Armstrong.—Life of Sir Henry Vane, by C. W. Upham.

Vol. V. Life of John Eliot, the Apostle of the Indians, by Convers Francis.

Vol. VI. Life of William Pinkney, by Henry Wheaton.—Life of William Ellery, by E. T. Channing.—Life of Cotton Mather, by Wm. B. O. Peabody.

Vol. VII. Life of Sir William Phips, by Francis Bowen.—Life of Israel Putnam, by Wm. B. O. Peabody.—Memoir of Lucretia Maria Davidson, by Miss Sedgwick.—Life of David Rittenhouse, by James Renwick.

Vol. VIII. Life of Jonathan Edwards, by Samuel Miller.—Life of David Brainerd, by Wm. B. O. Peabody.

Vol. IX. Life of Baron Steuben, by Francis Bowen.—Life of Sebastian Cabot, by Charles Hayward, Jr.—Life of William Eaton, by Cornelius C. Felton.

Vol. X. Life of Robert Fulton, by J. Renwick.—Life of Henry Hudson, by Henry R. Cleveland.—Life of Joseph Warren, by Alexander H. Everett.—Life of Father Marquette, by Jared Sparks.

Lives of Jay and Hamilton. By James Renwick. 18mo. Portrait.—45 cents.

The Life of De Witt Clinton. By James Renwick, LL.D. 18mo. Portrait.

Life of Commodore Oliver H. Perry. By Lieut. A. Slidell Mackenzie, Author of "A Year in Spain," &c. 2 vols. 18mo. Portrait.

A Life of Washington. By J. K. Paulding, Esq. 2 vols. 18mo. Engravings.

The Life and Works of Dr. Franklin. New Edition. 2 vols. 18mo. With a Portrait on steel.

The Pursuit of Knowledge under Difficulties; its Pleasures and Rewards. Illustrated by Memoirs of Eminent Men. 2 vols. 18mo.

The Life and Travels of Mungo Park. With the Substance of later Discoveries relative to his lamented Fate and the Termination of the Niger. 18mo. Engravings.

The Life and Works of Dr. Johnson. By the Rev. Wm. P. Page. 2 vols. 18mo. Portrait.

Distinguished Men of Modern Times. 2 vols. 18mo.

The Life and Works of Dr Oliver Goldsmith. By Washington Irving 2 vols. 18mo. Portrait.

Plutarch's Lives. Translated from the original Greek, with Notes, critical and historical, and a Life of Plutarch. By John Langhorne, D.D., and William Langhorne, A.M. A new Edition, carefully revised and corrected. In one volume 8vo. With Plates. Sheep extra.—$2 00.

The same work in 4 elegant 12mo volumes, large type. Sheep extra.—$3 50.

Letters and Journals of Lord Byron. With Notices of his Life. By Thomas Moore, Esq. 2 vols. 8vo. With a Portrait. Sheep.—$2 75.

Memoirs of Aaron Burr. With Miscellaneous Selections from his Correspondence. By Matthew L. Davis. 2 vols. 8vo. Portraits.

Private Journal of Aaron Burr, during his Residence in Europe, with Selections from his Correspondence. Edited by M. L. Davis. 2 vols. 8vo.—$4 50.

Memoirs of the Life and Correspondence of Mrs. Hannah More. By William Roberts, Esq. 2 vols. 12mo. Portrait.

Lives of the Signers of the Declaration of Independence. By N. Dwight. 12mo.—75 cents.

The Life and Adventures of Bruce, the African Traveller. By Major Sir Francis B. Head. 18mo. Portrait. —45 cents.

The Life and Death of Lord Edward Fitzgerald. By Thomas Moore. 2 vols. 12mo.

Traits of the Tea-Party; being a Memoir of George R. T. Hewes, one of the Last of its Survivers. With a History of that Transaction; Reminiscences of the Massacre and the Siege, and other Stories of Old Times. By a Bostonian. 18mo. Portrait.—63 cents.

Wonderful Characters; comprising Memoirs and Anecdotes of the most remarkable Persons of every Age and Nation. By Henry Wilson. 8vo. Engravings.

The Life of John Jay; with Selections from his Correspondence and Miscellaneous Papers. By his Son, William Jay. 2 vols. 8vo. Portrait.—$5 00.

A Memoir of the Life of William Livingston, Member of Congress in 1774, 1775, and 1776; Delegate to the Federal Convention in 1787, and Governor of the State of New-Jersey from 1776 to 1790. With Extracts from his Correspondence, and Notices of various Members of his Family. By T. Sedgwick, Jr. 8vo. Portrait.—$2 00.

Sketches of the Life and Character of the Rev. Lemuel Haynes, A.M. By Timothy Mather Cooley, D.D. With some Introductory Remarks by Wm. B. Sprague, D.D. 12mo. Portrait. —90 cents.

Memoirs of the Duchess d'Abrantes (Madame Junot). 8vo. Portrait.—$1 38.

Records of my Life. By John Taylor, Author of "Monsieur Tonson." 8vo. —$1 50.

Memoirs of Lucien Bonaparte (Prince of Canino). 12mo.

The Life and Remains of Edward Daniel Clarke. By the Rev. William Otter, A.M., F.L.S. 8vo.

The History of Virgil A. Stewart, and his Adventures in capturing and exposing the Great "Western Land Pirate" and his Gang, in Connexion with the Evidence; also of the Trials, Confessions, and Execution of a Number of Murrell's Associates in the State of Mississippi during the Summer of 1835, and the Execution of five professional Gamblers by the Citizens of Vicksburg, on the 6th of July, 1835. Compiled by H. R. Howard. 12mo.

The Religious Opinions and Character of Washington. By Rev. E. C. M'Guire. 12mo.

Lives of the Necromancers; or, an Account of the most Eminent Persons in successive Ages, who have claimed for themselves, or to whom has been imputed by others, the Exercise of Magical Power. By William Godwin. 12mo.

A Life of George Washington. In Latin Prose. By Francis Glass, A.M., of Ohio. Edited by J. N. Reynolds. 12mo. Portrait.

Life of Edmund Kean. By Barry Cornwall. 12mo.

Life of Mrs. Siddons. By Thomas Campbell. 12mo. With a Portrait —70 cents.

The Life of Wiclif. By Charles Webb Le Bas, A.M. 18mo. Portrait.—50 cents.

The Life of Archbishop Cranmer. By Charles Webb Le Bas, A.M. 2 vols. 18mo. Portrait.

Luther and the Lutheran Reformation. By the Rev. John Scott, A.M. 2 vols. 18mo. Portraits.

The Life of Andrew Jackson, President of the United States of America. By William Cobbett, M.P. 18mo. With a Portrait.

Matthias and his Impostures; or, the Progress of Fanaticism. Illustrated in the Extraordinary Case of Robert Matthews and some of his Forerunners and Disciples. By William L. Stone. 18mo.

Sketches and Eccentricities of Colonel David Crockett. 12mo.

Anecdotes of Sir Walter Scott. By the Ettrick Shepherd. With a Life of the Author, by S. Dewitt Bloodgood, Esq. 12mo.

The Life of Baron Cuvier. By Mrs. Lee. 12mo.

The Life, Character, and Literary Labours of Samuel Drew, A.M. By his eldest Son. 12mo.

My Imprisonments: Memoirs of Silvio Pellico da Saluzzo. Translated from the Italian. By Thomas Roscoe. 12mo.

The Life of Napoleon Bonaparte. By J. G. Lockhart, Esq. 2 vols. 18mo. Portraits.

The Life of Nelson. By Robert Southey, LL.D. 18mo. Portrait.—45 cents.

The Life and Actions of Alexander the Great. By the Rev. J. Williams. 18mo. Map.

The Life of Lord Byron. By John Galt, Esq. 18mo.

The Life of Mohammed, Founder of the Religion of Islam, and of the Empire of the Saracens. By the Rev. George Bush, of New-York. 18mo. With Engravings.

The Life and Times of George the Fourth. With Anecdotes of distinguished Persons of the last Fifty Years. By Rev. George Croly. 18mo.

Lives of the most eminent Painters and Sculptors. By Allan Cunningham, Esq. 5 vols. 18mo. Portraits.—$2 10.

The Life of Mary, Queen of Scots. By Henry Glassford Bell, Esq. 2 vols. 18mo. Portrait.

Life of Sir Isaac Newton. By Sir David Brewster, K.B., LL.D., F.R.S. 18mo. Engravings.

Memoirs of the Empress Josephine By John S. Memes, LL.D. 18mo. Portraits.

The Court and Camp of Bonaparte. 18mo. Portrait.

Lives and Voyages of Drake, Cavendish, and Dampier. Including an Introductory View of the earlier Discoveries in the South Seas, and the History of the Bucaniers. 18mo. Portraits.

Memoirs of Celebrated Female Sovereigns. By Mrs. Jameson. 2 vols. 18mo.

Lives of Celebrated Travellers. By James Augustus St. John. 3 vols. 18mo.

Life of Frederick the Second, King of Prussia, by Lord Dover. 2 vols. 18mo. Portrait.

Indian Biography; or, an Historical Account of those Individuals who have been distinguished among the North American Natives as Orators, Warriors, Statesmen, and other Remarkable Characters. By B. B. Thatcher, Esq. 2 vols. 18mo. Portrait.

History of Charlemagne. To which is prefixed an Introduction, comprising the History of France from the earliest Period to the Birth of Charlemagne. By G. P. R. James. 18mo. Portrait.

The Life of Oliver Cromwell. By the Rev. M. Russell, LL.D. 2 vols. 18mo. Portrait.

Memoir of the Life of Peter the Great. By John Barrow, Esq. 18mo. Portrait.

Lives of the Apostles and Early Martyrs of the Church. 18mo. Engravings.

Sketches of the Lives of Distinguished Females. Written for Young Ladies, with a View to their Mental and Moral Improvement. By an American Lady. 18mo. Portrait, &c.—35 cents.

VOYAGES, TRAVELS, ETC.

Incidents of Travel in Central America, Chiapas, and Yucatan. By John L. Stephens, Esq., Author of "Incidents of Travel in Egypt, Arabia Petræa, and the Holy Land." With a Map and 80 Engravings. 2 vols. 8vo

Letters from Abroad to Kindred at Home. By Miss C. M. Sedgwick. 2 vols. 12mo.

Letters from the Old World. By a Lady of New-York. 2 vols. 12mo.—$1 75.

Travels in the United States. By J. S. Buckingham, Esq. 2 vols. 8vo.

The Nestorians; or, the Lost Tribes. Containing Evidence of their Identity, an Account of their Manners, Customs, and Ceremonies, together with Sketches of Travel in Ancient Assyria, Armenia, Media, and Mesopotamia, and Illustrations of Scripture Prophecy. By Asahel Grant, M.D. 12mo. Map.—$1 00.

Embassy to the Eastern Courts of Siam, Cochin-China, and Muscat. By Edmund Roberts. 8vo.—$1 75.

Voyage of the United States Frigate Potomac, under the Command of Com. John Downes, during the Circumnavigation of the Globe, in the Years 1831, 1832, 1833, and 1834; including a particular Account of the Engagement at Quallah-Battoo, on the coast of Sumatra; with all the official Documents relating to the same. By J. N. Reynolds. 8vo. Illustrated with ten Steel Engravings. Fancy muslin.—$3 25.

Voyages for the Discovery of a Northwest Passage from the Atlantic to the Pacific, and Narrative of an Attempt to reach the North Pole. By W. E. Parry, Capt. R.N., F.R.S. 2 vols. 18mo. Engravings.

Travels in Europe; viz., in England Ireland, Scotland, France, Italy, Switzerland, some parts of Germany, and the Netherlands, during the Years 1835 and '36. By Wilbur Fisk, D.D. 8vo. With Engravings. Sheep extra.—$3 25.

The Life and Adventures of Bruce, the African Traveller. By Major Sir F. B. Head. 18mo. Portrait.

Incidents of Travel in Egypt, Arabia Petræa, and the Holy Land. By an American. 2 vols. 12mo. Twelfth Edition. Engravings.—$1 75.

Two Years before the Mast; a Personal Narrative of Life at Sea. By R. H. Dana, Jr. 18mo.

The Far West; or, a Tour beyond the Mountains. 2 vols. 12mo.—$1 50.

Incidents of Travel in Greece, Turkey, Russia, and Poland. By the Author of "Incidents of Travel in Egypt, Arabia Petræa, and the Holy Land." 2 vols. 12mo. Seventh Edition. Engravings.—$1 75.

Great Britain, France, and Belgium. A short Tour in 1835. By Heman Humphrey, D.D. 2 vols. 12mo.—$1 75.

The Life and Travels of Mungo Park. With the Substance of later Discoveries relative to his lamented Fate and the Termination of the Niger. 18mo. Engravings.

Retrospect of Western Travel. By Miss H. Martineau. 2 vols. 12mo.—$1 40.

A Year in Spain. By a Young American. 3 vols. 12mo. Vignette Embellishments. Fancy muslin.—$2 25.

Spain Revisited. By the Author of "A Year in Spain." 2 vols. 12mo. Engravings. Fancy muslin.—$1 75.

The American in England. By the Author of "A Year in Spain." 2 vols. 12mo. Fancy muslin.—$1 50.

Travels and Researches in Caffraria; describing the Character, Customs, and Moral Condition of the Tribes inhabiting that Portion of Southern Africa. By Stephen Kay. 12mo. Maps, &c.—85 cents.

A Narrative of Four Voyages to the South Sea, North and South Pacific Ocean, Chinese Sea, Ethiopic and Southern Atlantic Ocean, and Antarctic Ocean. From the Year 1822 to 1831. Comprising an Account of some valuable Discoveries, including the Massacre Islands, where thirteen of the Author's Crew were massacred and eaten by Cannibals. By Capt. Benjamin Morrell, Jun. 8vo.—$1 88.

Narrative of a Voyage to the South Seas, in 1829-31. By Abby Jane Morrell, who accompanied her husband, Capt. B. Morrell, Jun., of the Schooner Antarctic. 12mo.—63 cts

The Narrative of Arthur Gordon Pym of Nantucket. Comprising the Details of a Mutiny and atrocious Butchery on board the American

Brig Grampus, on her way to the South Seas, in the Month of June, 1827. 12mo.

Narrative of an Expedition through the Upper Mississippi to Itasca Lake, the actual Source of this River; embracing an Exploratory Trip through the St. Croix and Burntwood (or Broulé) Rivers. By Henry Schoolcraft. 8vo. With Maps.

Paris and the Parisians, in 1835. By Frances Trollope. 8vo. Engravings.

Sketches of Turkey in 1831 and 1832. By an American. 8vo. Engravings. —$2 00.

A Narrative of the Visit to the American Churches, by the Deputation from the Congregational Union of England and Wales. By Andrew Reed, D.D., and James Matheson, D.D. 2 vols. 12mo.

Four Years in Great Britain. By Calvin Colton. 12mo.

Visits and Sketches at Home and Abroad. With Tales and Miscellanies now first collected, and a new Edition of the "Diary of an Ennuyée." By Mrs. Jameson. 2 vols. 12mo.—$1 00.

Letters from the Ægean. By James Emerson, Esq. 8vo.—75 cents.

The Southwest. By a Yankee. In 2 vols. 12mo.—$1 50.

The Rambler in North America. By C. J. Latrobe, Author of the "Alpenstock," &c. 2 vols. 12mo.—$1 10.

The Rambler in Mexico. By Charles Joseph Latrobe. 12mo.—65 cents.

Constantinople and its Environs. In a Series of Letters, exhibiting the actual State of the Manners, Customs, and Habits of the Turks, Armenians, Jews, and Greeks, as modified by the policy of Sultan Mahmoud. By an American long resident at Constantinople (Commodore Porter). 2 vols. 12mo.—$1 50.

A Winter in the West. By a New-Yorker (C. F. Hoffman, Esq.). In 2 vols. 12mo.—$1 50.

Polynesian Researches, during a Residence of nearly eight Years in the Society and Sandwich Islands. By William Ellis. 4 vols. 12mo. With Maps, &c.—$2 50.

A Home Tour through the Manufacturing Districts of England. By Sir George Head. 12mo.—$1 13.

The Tourist, or Pocket Manual for Travellers on the Hudson River, the Western Canal and Stage Road to Niagara Falls, down Lake Ontario and the St. Lawrence to Montreal and Quebec. Comprising also the Routes to Lebanon, Ballston, and Saratoga Springs. 18mo. With a Map.—38 cents.

Things as they are; or, Notes of a Traveller through some of the Middle and Northern States. 12mo. Engravings.—75 cents.

Observations on Professions, Literature, Manners, and Emigration in the United States and Canada. By the Rev. Isaac Fidler. 12mo.—60 cents.

Narrative of Voyages to Explore the Shores of Africa, Arabia, and Madagascar; performed in H. M. Ships Leven and Barracouta, under the Direction of Captain W. F. W. Owen, R.N. 2 vols. 12mo.—$1 13.

A Subaltern's Furlough: Descriptive of Scenery in various Parts of the United States, Upper and Lower Canada, New-Brunswick, and Nova Scotia, during the Summer and Autumn of 1832. By E. T. Coke, Lieutenant of the 45th Regiment. 2 vols. 12mo.

Narrative of Discovery and Adventure in Polar Seas and Regions. With Illustrations of their Climate, Geology, and Natural History, and an Account of the Whale-Fishery. By Professors Leslie and Jameson, and Hugh Murray, Esq. 18mo. Maps, &c.

Narrative of Discovery and Adventure in Africa. From the earliest Ages to the present Time. With Illustrations of its Geology, Mineralogy, and Zoology. By Professor Jameson, and J. Wilson and Hugh Murray, Esqrs. 18mo. Engravings.

Description of Pitcairn's Island and its Inhabitants. With an Authentic Account of the Mutiny of the Ship Bounty, and of the subsequent Fortunes of the Mutineers. By J. Barrow, Esq. 18mo. Engravings.—45 cents.

Journal of an Expedition to Explore the Course and Termination of the Niger. With a Narrative of a Voyage down that River to its Termination. By Richard and John Lander. 2 vols. 18mo. Engravings.

The Travels and Researches of Alexander Von Humboldt; being a condensed Narrative of his Journeys in the Equinoctial Regions of America, and in Asiatic Russia; together with Analyses of his more important Investigations. By W. Macgillivray, A.M. 18mo. Engravings.

Lives and Voyages of Drake, Cavendish, and Dampier. Including an Introductory View of the earlier Discoveries in the South Seas, and the History of the Bucaniers. 18mo. Portraits.

Lives of Celebrated Travellers. By J. A. St. John. 3 vols. 18mo.—$1 25.

Historical View of the Progress of Discovery on the Northern Coasts of North America. From the earliest Period to the present Time. By P. F. Tytler, Esq. With descriptive Sketches of the Natural History of the North American Regions. By Professor Wilson. 18mo. With a Map, &c.

An Historical Account of the Circumnavigation of the Globe, and of the Progress of Discovery in the Pacific Ocean, from the Voyage of Magellan to the Death of Cook. 18mo. With numerous Engravings.

Perils of the Sea; being Authentic Narratives of Remarkable and Affecting Disasters upon the Deep. With Illustrations of the Power and Goodness of God in wonderful Preservations. 18mo. Engravings.

Caroline Westerley; or, the Young Traveller from Ohio. By Mrs. Phelps (formerly Mrs. Lincoln) 18mo. Engravings.

An Improved Map of the Hudson River, with the Post Roads between New-York and Albany.

THEOLOGY, ETC.

BARNES' NOTES. Viz.,

On the Gospels. New and Enlarged Edition, illustrated by numerous Engravings, and a Map of Jerusalem by Catherwood. 2 vols.—$1 50.

On the Acts of the Apostles.—75 cents.

On Romans.—75 cents.

On First Corinthians.—75 cents.

On Second Corinthians and Galatians.—75 cents.

Questions to the above in separate volumes.—25 cents per vol.

Mosheim's Institutes of Ecclesiastical History, Ancient and Modern, in four Books, much Corrected, Enlarged, and Improved, from the Primary Authorities. A new and literal Translation from the original Latin, with copious additional Notes, original and selected. By James Murdock, D.D. 3 vols. 8vo. Sheep extra.

Prideaux's Connexions; or, the Old and New Testaments connected, in the History of the Jews and neighbouring Nations, from the Declension of the Kingdoms of Israel and Judah to the Time of Christ. By Humphrey Prideaux, D.D. New Edition. In 2 vols. 8vo. Maps and Engravings. Sheep extra.—$3 75.

History of Christianity, from the Birth of Christ to the Abolition of Paganism in the Roman Empire. By Rev. H. H. Milman.

A History of the Church, from the earliest Ages to the Reformation. By the Rev. George Waddington, M.A. 8vo.—$1 75.

Beauties of the Bible, selected from the Old and New Testaments, with various Remarks and brief Dissertations. Designed for the Use of Schools and the Improvement of Youth. By Ezra Sampson. 18mo.

NATURAL THEOLOGY.

Paley's Natural Theology. With Illustrative Notes, by Henry Lord Brougham, F.R.S., and Sir Charles Bell, K.G.H., F.R.S. L. & E. With numerous Woodcuts. To which are added Preliminary Observations and Notes. By Alonzo Potter, D.D. 2 vols. 18mo,

On the Power, Wisdom, and Goodness of God, as manifested in the Adaptation of External Nature to the Moral and Intellectual Constitution of Man. By the Rev. Thomas Chalmers, D.D., Professor of Divinity in the University of Edinburgh. 12mo.

The Hand; its Mechanism and Vital Endowments as evincing Design. By Sir Charles Bell, K.G.H., F.R.S., L. & E. 12mo.

On Astronomy and General Physics By the Rev. William Whewell, M.A., F.R.S. 12mo.

Sacred History of the World, as displayed in the Creation and subsequent Events to the Deluge. At tempted to be philosophically considered in a Series of Letters to a Son. By Sharon Turner, F.S.A. 3 vols. 18mo.

Celestial Scenery; or, the Wonders of the Planetary System displayed. Illustrating the Perfections of Deity and a Plurality of Worlds. By T. Dick, LL.D. 18mo. Engravings.—45 cents.

The Sidereal Heavens, and other Subjects connected with Astronomy, as illustrative of the Character of the Deity, and an Infinity of Worlds. By Thomas Dick, LL.D. 18mo. Engravings.

Sermons. By Rev. John Summerfield. Edited by Rev. Daniel Smith. 8vo.

A Narrative of Events connected with the Rise and Progress of the Protestant Episcopal Church in Virginia. To which is added an Appendix, containing the Journals of the Conventions in Virginia from the Commencement to the present Time. By F. L. Hawks. 8vo.—$1 75.

History of the Bible. By the Rev. G. R. Gleig. 2 vols. 18mo. Map.—80 cents.

The Life of Christ, in the Words of the Evangelists. A complete Harmony of the Gospel History of our Saviour. Small 4to. With thirty Engravings on Wood, by Adams.—$1 00.

Religion in its Relation to the Present Life. In a Series of Lectures, delivered before the Young Men's Association of Utica, by A. B. Johnson, and published at their request.

Evidence of the Truth of the Christian Religion, derived from the literal Fulfilment of Prophecy. By Rev. Alex. Keith. 12mo.

The Works of the Rev. Robert Hall, A.M. With a brief Memoir of his Life, by Dr. Gregory, and Observations on his Character as a Preacher, by the Rev. John Foster. Edited by Olinthus Gregory, LL.D. In 3 vols. 8vo. Portrait. Sheep extra.—$5 00.

The Miscellaneous Works of the Rev. John Wesley. 3 vols. 8vo.—$3 00.

A Dictionary of the Holy Bible. Containing an Historical Account of the Persons; a Geographical and Historical Account of the Places; a Literal, Critical, and Systematical Description of other Objects, whether Natural, Artificial, Civil, Religious, or Military; and an Explanation of the appellative Terms mentioned in the Old and New Testaments. By the Rev. John Brown. With a Life of the Author, and an Essay on the Evidences of Christianity. 8vo.—Sheep extra.—$1 75.

The Harmony of Christian Faith and Christian Character, and the Culture and Discipline of the Mind. By John Abercrombie, M.D. 18mo.

Protestant Jesuitism. By a Protestant. 12mo.—90 cents.

Sermons of the Rev. James Saurin, late Pastor of the French Church at the Hague. From the French, by the Rev. Robert Robinson, Rev. Henry Hunter, D.D., and Rev. Joseph Sutcliffe, A.M. A new Edition, with additional Sermons. Revised and corrected by the Rev. Samuel Burder, A.M. With a likeness of the Author and a general Index. From the last London Edition. With a Preface by the Rev. J. P. K. Henshaw, D.D. 2 vols. 8vo. Sheep extra.—$3 75.

Demonstration of the Truth of the Christian Religion. By Alex. Keith, D.D. 12mo. Plates.—$1 38.

A Treatise on the Millennium; in which the prevailing Theories on that Subject are carefully examined, and the true Scriptural Doctrine attempted to be elicited and established. By George Bush, A.M. 12mo.—65 cts.

The Consistency of the whole Scheme of Revelation with itself and with Human Reason. By Philip Nicholas Shuttleworth, D.D. 18mo.—45 cents.

A Concordance to the Holy Scriptures of the Old and New Testaments. By Rev. John Brown. 32mo.—30 cents.

The Comforter; or, Extracts selected for the Consolation of Mourners under the Bereavement of Friends and Relations. By a Village Pastor. 12mo.—45 cents.

Thoughts on the Religious State of the Country; with Reasons for preferring Episcopacy. By the Rev. Calvin Colton. 12mo.—60 cents.

Christianity independent of the Civil Government. 12mo.—60 cents.

Help to Faith; or, a Summary of the Evidences of the Genuineness, Authenticity, Credibility, and Divine Authority of the Holy Scriptures. By Rev. P. P. Sandford. 12mo.—60 cents.

Sunday Evenings; or, an easy Introduction to the Reading of the Bible.

By the Author of "The Infant Christian's First Catechism." In 3 vols. 18mo. Engravings.—94 cents.

Evidences of Christianity; or, Uncle Philip's Conversations with the Children about the Truth of the Christian Religion. 18mo. Engravings.—35 cents.

MEDICINE, SURGERY, ETC.

The Study of Medicine. By John Mason Good, M.D., F.R.S. Improved from the Author's Manuscripts, and by Reference to the latest Advances in Physiology, Pathology, and Practice. By Samuel Cooper, M.D., With Notes, by A. Sidney Doane, A.M., M.D. To which is prefixed a Sketch of the History of Medicine, from its Origin to the Commencement of the Nineteenth Century. By J. Bostock, M.D., F.R.S. 2 vols. 8vo. Sheep extra.—$5 00.

Midwifery Illustrated. By J. P. Maygrier, M.D. Translated from the French, with Notes, by A. Sidney Doane, A.M., M.D. With 82 Plates. 8vo. Fancy muslin.—$4 75

Surgery Illustrated. Compiled from the Works of Cutler, Hind, Velpeau, and Blasius. By A. Sidney Doane, A.M., M.D. With 52 Plates. 8vo. Fancy muslin.—$4 50.

An Elementary Treatise on Anatomy. By A. L. J. Bayle. Translated from the sixth French Edition, by A. Sidney Doane, A.M., M.D. 18mo.—87 cents.

Lexicon Medicum; or, Medical Dictionary. By R. Hooper, M.D. With Additions from American Authors, by Samuel Akerly, M.D. 8vo. Sheep extra.—$3 00.

A Dictionary of Practical Surgery. By S. Cooper, M.D. With numerous Notes and Additions, embracing all the principal American Improvements. By D. M' Reese, M.D. 8vo. Sheep extra.—$3 87.

Elements of the Etiology and Philosophy of Epidemics. By Joseph Mather Smith, M.D. 8vo.—$1 00.

A Treatise on Epidemic Cholera, as observed in the Duane-street Cholera Hospital, New-York, during its Prevalence there in 1834. By F. T. Ferris. 8vo. Plates.—$1 25

Directions for Invigorating and Prolonging Life; or, the Invalid's Oracle. By William Kitchiner, M.D. Improved by T. S. Barrett, M.D. 18mo. —40 cents.

The Economy of Health; or, the Stream of Human Life from the Cradle to the Grave. With Reflections, Moral, Physical, and Philosophical, on the Septennial Phases of Human Existence. By James Johnson. 18mo.—65 cents.

The Principles of Physiology applied to the Preservation of Health, and to the Improvement of Physical and Mental Education. By Andrew Combe, M.D. 18mo. Engravings. —50 cents.

The Philosophy of Living; or, the Way to enjoy Life and its Comforts. By Caleb Ticknor, A.M., M.D. 18mo. Engravings.—45 cents.

Animal Mechanism and Physiology; being a plain and familiar Exposition of the Structure and Functions of the Human System. Designed for the Use of Families and Schools. By John H. Griscom, M.D. 18mo. Engravings.—45 cents.

FOR SCHOOLS AND COLLEGES.

The Philosophy of Rhetoric. By George Campbell, D.D., F.R.S. A New Edition, with the Author's last Additions and Corrections.—$1 50.

A Life of George Washington. In Latin Prose. By Francis Glass, A.M., of Ohio. Edited by J. N. Reynolds. 12mo. Portrait.—$1 13.

Inquiries concerning the Intellectual Powers and the Investigation of Truth. By John Abercrombie, M.D., F.R.S. With Questions. 18mo.—45 cents.

The Philosophy of the Moral Feelings. By John Abercrombie, M.D., F.R.S. With Questions 18mo.—40 cents.

Paley's Natural Theology. With Illustrative Notes, by Henry Lord Brougham, F.R.S., and Sir Charles Bell, K.G.H., F.R.S. L. & E. With numerous Woodcuts. To which are added, Preliminary Observations and Notes. By Alonzo Potter, D.D. 2 vols. 18mo.

A Manual of Conchology. By T. Wyatt, M.A. Illustrated by 36 Plates, containing more than two hundred Types drawn from the Natural Shell. 8vo.—$2 75.

Familiar Illustrations of Natural Philosophy, selected principally from Daniell's Chemical Philosophy. By James Renwick, LL.D. 18mo. Engravings.

First Principles of Chemistry; being a familiar Introduction to the Study of that Science. By Professor Renwick. 18mo. Engravings.—75 cents.

The Elements of Geology, for Popular Use; containing a Description of the Geological Formations and Mineral Resources of the United States. By Charles A. Lee, A.M., M.D. 18mo. Engravings.—50 cents.

The Principles of Physiology applied to the Preservation of Health, and to the Improvement of Physical and Mental Education. By Andrew Combe, M.D. Enlarged Edition, with Questions. 18mo.—50 cents.

Applications of the Science of Mechanics to Practical Purposes. By James Renwick. Engravings.—90 cents.

Animal Mechanism and Physiology; being a plain and familiar Exposition of the Structure and Functions of the Human System. Designed for the Use of Families and Schools. By John H. Griscom, M.D. 18mo. Engravings.

Universal History, from the Creation of the World to the Decease of George III., 1820. By the Hon. Alexander Fraser Tytler and Rev. E. Nares, D.D. Edited by an American. In 6 vols. 18mo.—$2 70.

American History. By the Author of "American Popular Lessons." In 3 vols 18mo. Engravings.—$1 00.

The History of Greece. By Dr. Goldsmith. Edited by the Author of "American Popular Lessons," &c. 18mo.—45 cents.

The History of Rome. By Dr. Goldsmith. Edited by H. W. Herbert, Esq. 18mo.—45 cents.

An Elementary Treatise on Mechanics. Translated from the French of M. Boucharlat. With Additions and Emendations, designed to adapt it to the Use of the Cadets of the U. S. Military Academy. By Edward H. Courtenay. 8vo. Sheep.—$2 25.

Cobb's School Books. Including Walker's Dictionary, Explanatory Arithmetic, Nos. 1 and 2, North American Reader, &c.

A Table of Logarithms, of Logarithmic Sines, and a Traverse Table. 12mo. —50 cents.

*** Many other works, suitable for use as text-books, &c., and already largely introduced in schools and colleges, may be found under the heads of History, Biography, Natural Philosophy, and Natural History.

ANTHON'S SERIES OF CLASSICAL WORKS.

First Latin Lessons, containing the most important Parts of the Grammar of the Latin Language, together with appropriate Exercises in the translating and writing of Latin, for the Use of Beginners. By Charles Anthon, LL.D. 12mo.

First Greek Lessons, containing the most important Parts of the Grammar of the Greek Language, together with appropriate Exercises in the translating and writing of Greek. for the Use of Beginners. By Charles Anthon, LL.D. 12mo.

A Grammar of the Greek Language, for the Use of Schools and Colleges. By Charles Anthon, LL.D. 12mo.—90 cents.

Greek Reader. Principally from Jacobs. With English Notes, critical and explanatory, a Metrical Index to Homer and Anacreon, and a copious Lexicon. By Charles Anthon, LL.D. 12mo.—$1 75.

A System of Greek Prosody and Metre, for the Use of Schools and Colleges; together with the Choral Scanning of the Prometheus Vinctus of Æschylus, and the Ajax and Œdipus Tyrannus of Sophocles; to which are appended Remarks on the Indo-Germanic Analogies. By Charles Anthon, LL.D. 12mo.

Cæsar's Commentaries on the Gallic War; and the First Book of the Greek Paraphrase; with English Notes, critical and explanatory, Plans of Battles, Sieges, &c., and Historical, Geographical, and Archæological Indexes. By Charles Anthon, LL.D. 12mo. Map, Portrait, &c.—$1 40.

Sallust's Jugurthine War and Conspiracy of Catiline. With an English Commentary, and Geographical and Historical Indexes. By Charles Anthon, LL.D. Ninth Edition, corrected and enlarged. 12mo. Portrait.—88 cents.

Select Orations of Cicero. With English Notes, critical and explanatory, and Historical, Geographical, and Legal Indexes. By Charles Anthon, LL.D. A new Edition, with Improvements. 12mo. Portrait.—$1 20.

The Works of Horace. With English Notes, critical and explanatory. By Charles Anthon, LL D. New Edition, with corrections and improvements. 12mo.—$1 75.

A Classical Dictionary, containing an Account of all the Proper Names mentioned in Ancient Authors, and intended to elucidate all the important Points connected with the Geography, History, Biography, Archæology, and Mythology of the Greeks and Romans, together with a copious Chronological Table, and an Account of the Coins, Weights, and Measures of the Ancients, with Tabular Values of the same. By Charles Anthon, LL.D. 8vo.—$4 75.

A System of Latin Prosody and Metre. By Charles Anthon, LL.D. 12mo.

UPHAM'S PHILOSOPHICAL WORKS.

Elements of Mental Philosophy, abridged, and designed as a Text-book in Academies and High schools. By Thomas C. Upham. 12mo.—$1 25.

Elements of Mental Philosophy; embracing the two Departments of the Intellect and Sensibilities. By Thos. C. Upham, Professor of Mental and Moral Philosophy in Bowdoin College. 2 vols 12mo.—$2 50.

A Philosophical and Practical Treatise on the Will. By Thomas C. Upham. 12mo.—$1 25.

Outlines of Imperfect and Disordered Mental Action. By Thomas C. Upham. 18mo.—45 cents.

NATURAL PHILOSOPHY.

First Principles of Chemistry; being a familiar Introduction to the Study of that Science. By James Renwick, LL.D. 18mo. Engravings.—75 cents.

Chymistry applied to Agriculture. By M. le Compte Chaptal. With a preliminary Chapter on the Organization, Structure, &c., of Plants, by Sir Humphrey Davy. And an Essay on the Use of Lime as a Manure, by M. Puvis; with Introductory Observations to the same, by Professor Renwick. Translated and edited by Rev. William P. Page. 18mo.—50 cents.

An Elementary Treatise on Mechanics. Translated from the French of M. Boucharlat. With Additions and Emendations, designed to adapt it to the Use of the Cadets of the U. S. Military Academy. By Edward H. Courtenay. 8vo. Sheep.—$2 25.

Illustrations of Mechanics. By Professors Moseley and Renwick. 18mo. Engravings.—45 cents.

Celestial Scenery; or, the Wonders of the Planetary System displayed. Illustrating the Perfections of Deity and a Plurality of Worlds. By Thos. Dick, LL.D. 18mo. Engravings.—45 cents.

Letters on Natural Magic. Addressed to Sir Walter Scott. By Sir D. Brewster. 18mo. Engravings.

Familiar Illustrations of Natural Philosophy. Selected principally from Daniell's Chemical Philosophy. By James Renwick, LL.D. 18mo. Engravings.

On Astronomy and General Physics. By the Rev. William Whewell, M.A., F.R.S. 12mo.—50 cents

Applications of the Science of Mechanics to practical Purposes. By James Renwick, LL.D. 18mo. Illustrated by numerous Engravings.—90 cents.

The Earth: its Physical Condition and most Remarkable Phenomena. By W. Mullinger Higgins. 18mo. Engravings.

A Preliminary Discourse on the Study of Natural Philosophy. By John Frederic William Herschel, A.M., &c. 12mo.

The Sidereal Heavens, and other Subjects connected with Astronomy, as illustrative of the Character of the Deity, and an Infinity of Worlds. By Thomas Dick, LL.D. 18mo Engravings.

Letters of Euler on different Subjects of Natural Philosophy. Addressed to a German Princess. Translated by Hunter. With Notes, and a Life of Euler, by Sir David Brewster; with Additional Notes, by John Griscom, LL.D. With a Glossary of Scientific Terms. 2 vols. 18mo. Engravings.

NATURAL HISTORY.

The Book of Nature. By John Mason Good, M.D., F.R.S. To which is now prefixed, a Sketch of the Author's Life. 8vo. Sheep extra.—$1 25.

Natural History of Birds; their Architecture, Habits, &c. 18mo. With Engravings.

Natural History of Quadrupeds. 18mo. Engravings.

A Manual of Conchology, according to the System laid down by Lamarck, with the late Improvements by De Blainville. Exemplified and arranged for the Use of Students. By Thomas Wyatt, M.A. Illustrated by thirty-six Plates, containing more than two hundred Types drawn from the Natural Shell. 8vo.—$2 75.

The same Work, with coloured Plates.—$8 00.

The Hand; its Mechanism and Vital Endowments, as evincing Design. By Sir Charles Bell, K.G.H., F.R.S. L. & E. 12mo.—60 cents.

Vegetable Substances used for the Food of Man. 18mo. Engravings.—45 cents.

The Natural History of Insects. 2 vols. 18mo. Engravings.—90 cents.

A Popular Guide to the Observation of Nature; or, Hints of Inducement to the Study of Natural Productions and Appearances, in their Connexions and Relations. By Robert Mudie. 18mo. Engravings.

The Elephant as he exists in a Wild State, and as he has been made subservient, in Peace and in War, to the Purposes of Man. 18mo. Numerous Engravings.

The Elements of Geology, for popular Use; containing a Description of the Geological Formations and Mineral Resources of the United States. By Charles A. Lee, M.D. 18mo.—50 cents.

Natural History; or, Uncle Philip's Conversations with the Children about Tools and Trades among the Inferior Animals. 18mo. With Illustrative Engravings.

The American Forest; or, Uncle Philip's Conversations with the Children about the Trees of America. 18mo. Numerous Engravings.

POETRY, AND THE DRAMA.

Pocahontas, and other Poems. By Mrs. L. H. Sigowrney.

Powhatan. A Metrical Romance. By Seba Smith. 12mo.

The Dramatic Works and Poems of William Shakspeare. With Notes, original and selected, and introductory Remarks to each Play, by Samuel Weller Singer, F.S.A., and a Life of the Poet, by Charles Symmons, D.D. Complete in one volume, 8vo. Numerous Engravings. Sheep extra.—$3 50. Bound in 2 vols., $3 75.

The Dramatic Works of William Shakspeare, with the Corrections and Illustrations of Dr. Johnson, G. Steevens, and others. Revised by Isaac Reed, Esq. 6 vols. crown 8vo. With a Portrait and other Engravings. Fancy muslin.—$6 50.

Poems, by William Cullen Bryant. New Edition, enlarged. 12mo. With a Vignette. Fancy muslin.—$1 13.

The same Work, fancy muslin, gilt edges.—$1 25.

The same Work, bound in silk, gilt edges.—$1 37.

Poems, by Fitz-Greene Halleck. Now first collected. 12mo. Vignette.

Fanny, with other Poems. By Fitz-Greene Halleck. 12mo. With a Vignette.—$1 13.

Selections from American Poets. By W. C. Bryant. 18mo.

Selections from British Poets. By Fitz-Greene Halleck. 2 vols. 18mo.—90 cents.

Velasco. A Tragedy, in five Acts. By Epes Sargent. 12mo.

MISCELLANEOUS.

The Plays of Philip Massinger. In 3 vols. 18mo. Portrait.—$1 30.

The Dramatic Works of John Ford. With Notes, critical and explanatory. 2 vols. 18mo.—85 cents.

The Rivals of Este, and other Poems. By James G. Brooks and Mary E. Brooks. 12mo.—50 cents.

The Doom of Devorgoil, a Melo-Drama. Auchindrane; or, the Ayrshire Tragedy. By Sir Walter Scott. 12mo. —35 cents.

Virgil. The Eclogues translated by Wrangham, the Georgics by Sotheby, and the Æneid by Dryden. 2 vols. 18mo. Portrait.

Æschylus. Translated by the Rev. R Potter, M.A. 18mo.

Sophocles. Translated by Thomas Francklin, D.D. 18mo. Portrait.—45 cents.

Euripides. Translated by the Rev. R. Potter, M.A. 3 vols. 18mo. Portrait. —$1 30.

Horace. Translated by Philip Francis, D.D. With an Appendix, containing Translations of various Odes, &c., by Ben Jonson, Cowley, Milton, Dryden, Pope, Addison, Swift, Bentley, Chatterton, G. Wakefield, Porson, Byron, &c., and by some of the most eminent Poets of the present day. And

Phædrus. With the Appendix of Gudius. Translated by Christopher Smart, A.M. 2 vols. 18mo. Portrait. —90 cents.

Ovid. Translated by Dryden, Pope, Congreve, Addison, and others. 2 vols. 18mo. Portrait.

Homer. Translated by Alexander Pope, Esq. 3 vols. 18mo. Portrait. —$1 35.

Juvenal. Translated by Charles Badham, M D, F.R.S. New Edition. With an Appendix, containing Imitations of the Third and Tenth Satires, by Dr. Samuel Johnson. And

Persius. Translated by the Rt. Hon. Sir W. Drummond. 18mo. Portrait. —45 cents.

Pindar. Translated by the Rev. C. A. Wheelwright. And

Anacreon. Translated by Thomas Bourne, Esq. 18mo.

Dramatic Scenes from Real Life. By Lady Morgan. 2 vols. 12mo.—60 cents.

Richelieu: or, the Conspiracy. A Play. With Historical Odes. By Sir E. Lytton Bulwer. 12mo.

The Lady of Lyons. A Play. By Sir E. Lytton Bulwer. 12mo.

The Rebel, and other Tales. By Sir E. Lytton Bulwer. 12mo.—50 cents.

The Siamese Twins. A Satirical Tale of the Times, &c. By Sir E. Lytton Bulwer. 12mo.

The Sea-Captain; or, the Birthright. A Play. By Sir E. Lytton Bulwer. 12mo.

Blanche of Navarre. A Play. By G P. R. James, Esq. 12mo.

MISCELLANEOUS.

The Philosophical Emperor: a Political Experiment; or, the Progress of a False Position. Dedicated to the Whigs, Conservatives, Democrats, and Loco-focos, Individually and Collectively, of the United States. 18mo.

The Works of Joseph Addison. Complete in 3 vols. 8vo, embracing "The Spectator." Portrait. Sheep extra. —$5 50.

The Works of Henry Mackenzie, Esq. Complete in one vol. 12mo. Portrait. Fancy muslin.

The complete Works of Edmund Burke. With a Memoir. 3 vols. 8vo. Portrait. Sheep extra.

The Works of Charles Lamb. Complete—with his Life, &c., by Talfourd. 2 vols. 12mo. Portrait.— $3 25.

The Works of John Dryden, in Verse and Prose. With a Life, by the Rev. John Mitford. 2 vols. 8vo. Portrait. Sheep extra.

The Works of Hannah More. 7 vols. 12mo. Illustrations to each volume. Fancy muslin.

The same Work in 2 vols. royal 8vo, with Illustrations. Fancy muslin.— $3 50.

Also an Edition in one vol. royal 8vo, with a Portrait, &c. Fancy muslin. —$3 25. Sheep extra,

Elements of Mental Philosophy; embracing the two Departments of the Intellect and Sensibilities. By Thos. C. Upham, Professor of Mental and Moral Philosophy in Bowdoin College. 2 vols. 12mo.

A Philosophical and Practical Treatise

on the Will. By Thomas C. Upham. 12mo.

Outlines of Imperfect and Disordered Mental Action. 18mo.

The Farmer's Instructer; consisting of Essays, Practical Directions, and Hints for the Management of the Farm and the Garden. By Jesse Buel, Esq. 2 vols. 18mo.

A Treatise on Agriculture; comprising a concise History of its Origin and Progress; the present Condition of the Art abroad and at Home, and the Theory and Practice of Husbandry. To which is added, a Dissertation on the Kitchen and Fruit Garden. By Gen. John Armstrong. With Notes by Jesse Buel. 18mo.

American Husbandry; being a series of Essays, &c., designed for its Improvement, compiled principally from "The Cultivator" and "The Genesee Farmer," with Notes and Additions by Willis Gaylord and Luther Tucker, Editors of "The Cultivator," &c. 2 vols. 18mo. Engravings.

Algic Researches; comprising Inquiries respecting the Mental Characteristics of the North American Indians. First Series. Indian Tales and Legends. By Henry Rowe Schoolcraft. 2 vols. 12mo.

Infantry Tactics; or, Rules for the Exercise and Manœuvres of the United States' Infantry. New Edition. By Major-general Scott, U. S. Army. [Published by Authority.] 3 vols. 18mo. Plates.

The Fairy Book. 16mo. Illustrated with 81 Woodcuts by Adams. Fancy muslin, gilt edges.

Georgia Scenes. New Edition. With original Illustrations. 12mo. 90 cents.

The Life and Surprising Adventures of Robinson Crusoe, of York, Mariner. With a Biographical Account of De Foe. Illustrated with fifty characteristic Engravings by Adams. 12mo. Fancy muslin.

A new Hieroglyphical Bible, with 400 Cuts, by Adams. 16mo.—70 cents.

The Pilgrim's Progress. With a Life of Bunyan, by Robert Southey, LL.D. New and beautiful Edition, splendidly illustrated with 50 Engravings by Adams, and elegantly bound. 12mo.

The Life of Christ, in the Words of the Evangelists. A complete Harmony of the Gospel History of our Saviour. Small 4to. With 30 Engravings on Wood, by Adams.

Evenings at Home; or, the Juvenile Budget opened. By Dr. Aikin and Mrs. Barbauld. Small 4to. With 34 Engravings on Wood.

Essays on the Principles of Morality, and on the private and political Rights and Obligations of Mankind. By Jonathan Dymond. With a Preface, by the Rev. George Bush, M.A. 8vo. Fancy muslin.

The Percy Anecdotes. Revised Edition. To which is added, a valuable Collection of American Anecdotes, original and selected. 8vo. Portraits. Sheep extra.

English Synonymes. With copious Illustrations and Explanations, drawn from the best Writers. By George Crabb, M.A. 8vo. Sheep.

Selections from the Spectator: embracing the most interesting Papers by Addison, Steele, and others. 2 vols. 18mo

Political Economy. Its Objects stated and explained, and its Principles familiarly and practically illustrated. By Rev. Dr. Potter. 18mo.—50 cents.

Counsels to Young Men on the Formation of Character, and the Principles which lead to Success and Happiness in Life; being Addresses principally delivered at the Anniversary Commencements in Union College. By Eliphalet Nott, D.D., President of Union College. 18mo.

The Pleasures and Advantages of Science. By Lord Brougham, Professor Sedgwick, Gulian C. Verplanck, and Rev. Dr. Potter. 18mo.

The Family Instructer; or, a Manual of the Duties, &c., of Domestic Life. By a Parent. 18mo.

Anecdotes, Literary, Moral, Religious, and Miscellaneous. Compiled by the Rev. Messrs. Hoes and Way. 8vo. Sheep.

The Works of Lord Chesterfield, including his Letters to his Son. With a Life of the Author. 8vo.

Literary Remains of the late Henry Neele. 8vo.

Public and Private Economy. Illustrated by Observations made in Europe in 1836-7. By Theodore Sedgwick. In three Parts. 3 vols. 12mo.

The Writings of Robert C. Sands, in Prose and Verse. With a Memoir of the Author. 2 vols. 8vo. Portrait. —$3 75.

How to Observe.—Morals and Manners. By Harriet Martineau. 12mo. —43 cents.

Miniature Lexicon of the English Language. By Lyman Cobb. 48mo.— 50 cents.

Letters to Young Ladies. By Mrs. L. H. Sigourney. Third Edition, enlarged. 12mo.

Letters to Mothers. By Mrs. L. H. Sigourney. 12mo.

Letters, Conversations, and Recollections of the late S. T. Coleridge. 12mo.

Specimens of the Table-Talk of the late Samuel Taylor Coleridge. 12mo.— 70 cents.

Festivals, Games, and Amusements, Ancient and Modern. By Horatio Smith, Esq. With Additions, by Samuel Woodworth, Esq., of New-York. 18mo. Engravings.

A Treatise on Language; or, the Relations which Words bear to Things. By A. B. Johnson. 8vo.

France; Social, Literary, and Political. By H. L. Bulwer, Esq., M.P. 2 vols. 12mo.

England and the English. By Sir E. Lytton Bulwer, M.P. 2 vols. 12mo. 85 cents.

Practical Education. By Richard Lovell Edgeworth and Maria Edgeworth. 12mo.

Slavery in the United States. By J. K. Paulding, Esq. 18mo.

Letters on Demonology and Witchcraft. By Sir Walter Scott. 18mo. With an Engraving.

Inquiries concerning the Intellectual Powers, and the Investigation of Truth. By John Abercrombie, M.D., F.R.S. With Questions. 18mo.— 45 cents.

The Philosophy of the Moral Feelings. By John Abercrombie, M.D., F.R.S. With Questions. 18mo.

Lectures on General Literature, Poetry, &c. By James Montgomery. 18mo. —45 cents.

The Orations of Demosthenes. Translated by Thomas Leland, D.D. In 2 vols. 18mo. Portrait.

On the Improvement of Society by the Diffusion of Knowledge. By Thomas Dick, LL.D. 18mo. Engravings.— 45 cents.

Cicero. The Orations translated by Duncan, the Offices by Cockman, and the Cato and Lælius by Melmoth. 3 vols. 18mo. Portrait.

Indian Traits; being Sketches of the Manners, Customs, and Character of the North American Natives. By B. B. Thatcher, Esq. 2 vols. 18mo. Engravings.

The Swiss Family Robinson; or, Adventures of a Father and Mother and Four Sons on a Desert Island. The progress of the Story forming a clear Illustration of the first Principles of Natural History, and many Branches of Science which most immediately apply to the Business of Life. 2 vols. 18mo. Engravings.

The Son of a Genius. A Tale for the Use of Youth. By Mrs. Hofland. 18mo. Engravings.

The Young Crusoe; or, the Shipwrecked Boy. Containing an Account of his Shipwreck, and of his Residence alone upon an Uninhabited Island. By Mrs. Hofland. 18mo. Engravings.

Diary of a Physician. New Edition. 3 vols. 18mo.—$1 35.

The Clergyman's Orphan and other Tales. By a Clergyman. For the Use of Youth. 18mo. Engravings. —35 cents.

The Ornaments Discovered. By Mrs. Hughs. 18mo. Engravings. — 35 cents.

Uncle Philip's Conversations with the Children about the Whale-fishery and Polar Seas. 2 vols. 18mo. Engravings.

The Letters of the British Spy. By William Wirt, Esq. To which is prefixed, a Biographical Sketch of the Author. 12mo. Portrait.

Lost Greenland; or, Uncle Philip's Conversations with the Children about the Lost Colonies of Greenland. 18mo. With Engravings.— 35 cents.

The Poor Rich Man and the Rich Poor Man. By Miss Sedgwick. 18mo.— 45 cents.

Live and Let Live. By Miss Sedgwick. 18mo.

A Love Token for Children. By Miss Sedgwick. 18mo.

Stories for Young Persons. By Miss Sedgwick. 18mo.

The Lady of the Manor. By Mrs Sherwood. 4 vols. 12mo.

Roxobel. By Mrs. Sherwood. 3 vols. 18mo.

Frank. By Miss Edgeworth. 12mo.—90 cents.

Rosamond; and other Stories. By Miss Edgeworth. 12mo.

Harry and Lucy. By Miss Fdgeworth. 2 vols. 12mo.

The Parent's Assistant. By Miss Edgeworth. 12mo.—90 cents.

Scenes in our Parish. By a "Country Parson's" Daughter. 12mo. — 55 cents.

England and America. A Comparison of the Social and Political State of both Nations. 8vo.

No Fiction: a Narrative founded on Recent and Interesting Facts. By the Rev. Andrew Reed, D.D. New Edition. 12mo.

Martha; a Memorial of an only and beloved Sister. By the Rev. Andrew Reed, Author of "No Fiction." 12mo.

The Mechanic. By Rev. C. B. Tayler. 18mo.

The District School. By J. O. Taylor. 12mo.

Letters to Ada. By the Rev. Dr. Pise. 18mo.

Letters of J. Downing, Major, Downingville Militia, Second Brigade, to his Old Friend Mr. Dwight, of the New-York Daily Advertiser. 18mo. Engravings.

Domestic Duties, or Instructions to Young Married Ladies on the Management of their Households, and the Regulation of their Conduct in the various Relations and Duties of Married Life. By Mrs. W. Parkes. With Improvements. 12mo. — 75 cents.

Zion's Songster. Compiled by Rev. Thomas Mason. 48mo.

The Cook's Oracle and Housekeeper's Manual. Containing Receipts for Cookery, and Directions for Carving. With a Complete System of Cookery for Catholic Families. By William Kitchiner, M.D. 12mo.

Modern American Cookery. With a List of Family Medical Receipts, and a valuable Miscellany. By Miss P. Smith. 16mo.

Discourses and Addresses on Subjects of American History, Arts, and Literature. By Gulian C. Verplanck. 12mo

The Note-book of a Country Clergyman. 18mo.

FAMILY LIBRARY.

Abundantly illustrated by Maps, Portraits, and other Engravings on steel, copper, and wood. Bound uniformly, but each work sold separately.

Nos. 1, 2, 3. The History of the Jews. By the Rev. H. H. Milman.

4, 5. The Life of Napoleon Bonaparte By J. G. Lockhart, Esq.

6. The Life of Nelson. By Robert Southey, LL.D.

. The Life and Actions of Alexander the Great. By the Rev. J. Williams. 45 cents.

8, 74. The Natural History of Insects. —90 cents.

9. The Life of Lord Byron. By John Galt, Esq.

10. The Life of Mohammed. By the Rev. George Bush.

11. Letters on Demonology and Witchcraft. By Sir Walter Scott, Bart.—40 cents.

12, 13. History of the Bible. By the Rev. G. R. Gleig.

14. Narrative of Discovery and Adventure in the Polar Seas and Regions. By Professors Leslie and Jameson, and Hugh Murray, Esq.—

15. Life and Times of George the Fourth. By the Rev. George Croly. —45 cents.

16. Narrative of Discovery and Adventure in Africa. By Professor Jameson, and James Wilson and Hugh Murray, Esqrs.

17, 18, 19, 66, 67. Lives of the most eminent Painters and Sculptors. By Allan Cunningham, Esq.

20. History of Chivalry and the Crusades. By G. P. R. James, Esq.—45 cents.

21, 22. Life of Mary, Queen of Scots. By H. G. Bell, Esq.

23. A View of Ancient and Modern Egypt. By the Rev. M. Russell, LL.D.

24. History of Poland. By James Fletcher, Esq.

25. Festivals, Games, and Amusements. By Horatio Smith, Esq.

26. Life of Sir Isaac Newton. By Sir David Brewster, K.B., &c.

27. Palestine, or the Holy Land. By the Rev. M. Russell, LLD.—45 cents.
28. Memoirs of the Empress Josephine. By John S. Memes, LL D.
29. The Court and Camp of Bonaparte. —45 cents.
30. Lives and Voyages of Drake, Cavendish, and Dampier.
31. Description of Pitcairn's Island and its Inhabitants; with an Account of the Mutiny of the Ship Bounty, &c. By J. Barrow, Esq.
32, 72, 84. Sacred History of the World, as displayed in the Creation and subsequent Events to the Deluge. By Sharon Turner, F.S.A.
33, 34. Memoirs of Celebrated Female Sovereigns. By Mrs. Jameson.—80 cents.
35, 36. Journal of an Expedition to explore the Course and Termination of the Niger. By Richard and John Lander—90 cents.
37. Inquiries concerning the Intellectual Powers and the Investigation of Truth. By John Abercrombie.—45 cents.
38, 39, 40. Lives of Celebrated Travellers. By J. A. St. John.
41, 42. Life of Frederic the Second, King of Prussia. By Lord Dover.—90 cents.
43, 44. Sketches from Venetian History. By the Rev. E. Smedley, M.A.—90 cents.
45, 46. Indian Biography; or, an Historical Account of those Individuals who have been distinguished among the North American Natives as Orators, Warriors, Statesmen, and other remarkable Characters. By B. B. Thatcher, Esq.
47, 48, 49. Historical and Descriptive Account of British India. By Hugh Murray, Esq., James Wilson, Esq., R. K. Greville, LL.D., Whitelaw Ainslie, M.D., William Rhind, Esq., Professor Jameson, Professor Wallace, and Captain Clarence Dalrimple.
50. Letters on Natural Magic. By Dr. Brewster.
51, 52. History of Ireland. By W. C. Taylor, Esq.
53. Historical View of the Progress of Discovery on the Northern Coasts of North America. By P. F. Tytler, Esq.
54. The Travels and Researches of Alexander Von Humboldt. By W. Macgillivray, A.M.
55, 56. Letters of Euler on Different Subjects of Natural Philosophy. Translated by Hunter. With Notes, &c., by Sir David Brewster and John Griscom, LL.D.
57. A Popular Guide to the Observatics of Nature. By R. Mudie.
58. The Philosophy of the Moral Feelings. By J. Abercrombie.—40 cents.
59. On the Improvement of Society by the Diffusion of Knowledge. By Thomas Dick, LL.D.
60. History of Charlemagne. By G. P. R. James, Esq.
61. Nubia and Abyssinia. By the Rev. M. Russell, LL.D
62, 63. Life of Oliver Cromwell. By the Rev. M. Russell, LL.D.—90 cents.
64. Lectures on General Literature, Poetry, &c. By James Montgomery. —45 cents.
65. Memoir of the Life of Peter the Great. By J. Barrow, Esq.
66, 67. The Lives of the most eminent Painters and Sculptors. By Allan Cunningham. 2d Series.
68, 69. The History of Arabia. By Andrew Crichton.
70. Historical and Descriptive Account of Persia. By James B. Fraser, Esq. —45 cents.
71. The Principles of Physiology applied to the Preservation of Health, and to the Improvement of Physical and Mental Education. By Andrew Combe, M.D.
72. Sacred History of the World. By S. Turner, F.S.A. Vol.2.
73. History and Present Condition of the Barbary States. By the Rev. M. Russell, LL.D.
74. The Natural History of Insects. Vol. 2.
75, 76. A Life of Washington. By J. K. Paulding. Esq.
77. The Philosophy of Living. By Caleb Ticknor, A.M.
78. The Earth: its Physical Condition and most remarkable Phenomena. By W. M. Higgins.
79 A Compendious History of Italy. Translated by N. Greene.
80, 81. The Chinese. By John Francis Davis, F.R.S.
82. Historical Account of the Circumnavigation of the Globe, &c.
83. Celestial Scenery; or, the Wonders of the Planetary System displayed. By Thomas Dick, LL.D.
84. Sacred History of the World. By S. Turner. F.S A. Vol. 3.
85. Animal Mechanism and Physiology. By John H. Griscom, M.D.—45 cents.
86, 87, 88, 89, 90, 91. Universal History. By the Hon. Alexander Fraser Tytler and Rev. F. Nares.

92, 93. The Life and Works of Dr. Franklin.

94, 95. The Pursuit of Knowledge under Difficulties; its Pleasures and Rewards.

96, 97. Paley's Natural Theology. With Notes, &c., by Henry Lord Brougham, Sir Charles Bell, and A. Potter, D.D.

98. Natural History of Birds; their Architecture, Habits, &c.

89. The Sidereal Heavens, and other Subjects connected with Astronomy. By Thomas Dick, LL.D.

100. Outlines of Imperfect and Disordered Mental Action. By Professor Upham.

101, 102. Historical and Descriptive Account of British America. By Hugh Murray, F.R.S.E.

103. Outline History of the Fine Arts. By Benson J. Lossing.

104. Natural History of Quadrupeds.—45 cents.

105. Life and Travels of Mungo Park.—45 cents.

106. Two Years before the Mast. By R. H. Dana, Jr.

107, 108. Voyages for the Discovery of a Northwest Passage from the Atlantic to the Pacific, &c. By Sir W. E. Parry, Capt. R.N., F.R.S.

109, 110. Life and Works of Dr. Johnson. By the Rev. Wm. P. Page.—90 cents.

111 Selections from American Poets. By W. C. Bryant.

112, 113. Selections from British Poets. By Fitz-Greene Halleck.

114, 115, 116, 117, 118. History of England. By Thomas Keightley.

119, 120. History of the United States. By the Hon. S. Hale. (An original work, written expressly for this Library.)

121, 122. The Life and Works of Dr. Oliver Goldsmith. By Washington Irving.

123, 124. Distinguished Men of Modern Times.

125. Life of De Witt Clinton. By James Renwick, LL.D.

126, 127. Life of Commodore Oliver H. Perry. By Lieut. A. Slidell Mackenzie.

128. Life and Adventures of Bruce, the African Traveller. By Major Sir Francis B. Head.

129. Lives of John Jay and Alexander Hamilton. By James Renwick.—45 cents.

130. The Martyrs of Science; or, the Lives of Galileo, Tycho Brahe, and Kepler. By Sir David Brewster, K.H. 18mo.

131. An Historical and Descriptive Account of Iceland, Greenland, and the Faroe Islands. 18mo. Maps and Engravings.

132. Manners and Customs of the Japanese, in the Nineteenth Century. From the Accounts of recent Dutch Residents in Japan, and from the German Work of DR. PH. FR. Von Siebold. 18mo.—45 cents.

133. History of Connecticut. By Theodore Dwight, Jr. 18mo. 45 cents.

134, 135. Ruins of Ancient Cities; with General and Particular Accounts of their Rise, Fall, and present Condition. By Charles Bucke. 2 vols. 18mo.

CLASSICAL LIBRARY.

With Portraits on steel. Bound uniformly, but each work sold separately.

Nos. 1, 2. Xenophon. (Anabasis, translated by Edward Spelman, Esq., Cyropædia, by the Hon. M. A. Cooper.)

3, 4. The Orations of Demosthenes. Translated by Thomas Leland, D.D.—85 cents.

5. Sallust. Translated by William Rose, M.A.

6, 7. Cæsar. Translated by William Duncan.

8, 9, 10. Cicero. The Orations translated by Duncan, the Offices by Cockman, and the Cato and Lælius by Melmoth.

11, 12. Virgil. The Eclogues translated by Wrangham, the Georgics by Sotheby, and the Æneid by Dryden.—90 cents.

13. Æschylus. Translated by the Rev. R. Potter, M.A.

14. Sophocles. Translated by Thomas Francklin, D.D.

15, 16, 17. Euripides. Translated by the Rev. R. Potter, M.A.

18, 19. Horace. Translated by Philip Francis, D.D. With an Appendix, containing Translations of various Odes, &c., by Ben Jonson, Cowley, Milton, Dryden, &c. And Phædrus. With the Appendix of Gudius. Translated by Christopher Smart, A.M

20, 21. Ovid. Translated by Dryden, Pope, Congreve, Addison, and others.—90 cents.

22, 23. Thucydides. Translated by William Smith, A.M.

www.ingramcontent.com/pod-product-compliance
Lightning Source LLC
LaVergne TN
LVHW020242110826
845151LV00003B/1011
* 9 7 8 1 4 2 5 5 2 8 6 3 8 *